The Compleat Music Teacher

Ruth Edwards is

> *Chairman, Preparatory Piano Department*
> *Chairman, Piano Pedagogy and Teacher's Training Department*
> The Cleveland Institute of Music
>
> *Music Therapist*
> Ingleside Psychiatric Hospital, Cleveland

and the author of

> *First Steps in Music*, by Ruth Edwards and Eric Simon. Edward Marks
> *Fifteen American Folk Songs for Children.* Summy-Birchard

The Compleat Music Teacher
by Ruth Edwards

> Noght a word spak he more than was nede, and that was said in form and reverence, and short and quik, and ful of hy sentence. Sowninge in moral vertue was his speech, and gladly wolde he lern and gladly teche.
> Chaucer

Geron-X, Inc.
Los Altos, California

© Copyright 1970 by Ruth Edwards
All rights reserved
No part of this book may be reproduced in any form without written
  permission from the author or publisher, except by a reviewer who
  may quote brief passages in a review to be printed in a magazine or
  newspaper

Published by Geron-X, Inc., Box 1108, Los Altos, Calif. 94022

Standard Book Number 87672-106-4
Library of Congress Catalog Card Number 79-109368

Printed in the United States of America

This Book Is Dedicated to

Irene	Lydia
Joel	John
Danny	Timothy
Gerald	Bobby
Ronald	Christiane
Eugene	Stephanie
Marilyn	Cecelie
Anita	Luda
Mary	Abby
Diane	Michael
Lisa	Shari
Barbara	Stephen
Myroslava	Christine
Edith	Nona

They have taught me more than I have ever taught them.

Foreword

We hear that someone teaches history or swimming or music—but that is a figure of speech. What he is really teaching is people. We may admit that history, swimming, or music are "subjects"; but the objects are always human beings. To get the object to embrace and to absorb, to be penetrated and suffused by the subject, that is the purpose of teaching; but it is the object, the human being, that always presents the greater difficulty, the greater challenge, the greater mystery.

Eager young American physicians have gone abroad to work under some celebrated European specialist; often they have come back enhanced in knowledge, but complaining that the great professor seemed to be more interested in the disease than in the patient. Music teachers, especially those themselves possessed of great skill and knowledge, tend to fail in the same way; they are more interested in music than in the pupil. It is against this propensity that Ruth Edwards aims to launch a counterthrust.

I particularly like her concern with "empathy." It seems a pity that the well-understood idea, so fundamental in all human relations, should be expressed by a word which sounds so medical and so foreign. Perhaps some day we may have a familiar English word for it, something like the German "Einfühlung."

Try—do not pretend—to be a seven-year-old child without any adult resources of experience and practice, and then face yourself with a simple problem of coordination that you have never before met with. Try—not pretend—to be a fifteen-year-old, uncertain of whether you are a child or an adult, to withstand the first impact of your awakening and growth, and then set yourself the task of working steadily and of controlling your enthusiasms and your repulsions. If you can do these things successfully, you have the gift of empathy. Ruth Edwards has it.

Her book is based on many years of successful experience as a teacher of piano. It is full of specific suggestions which other teachers will accept with profit. Those who have talent and lack the skill will find compact, a rich experience which will serve and save them much. Yet teaching remains an art, not a series of grips and passes. All will do well to follow the author's advice, though that will not enable them to achieve her artistry cheaply. Some of us, practitioners of music who know all the ropes as teachers, performers, and critics, have felt we could do no better for our children's musical education than to entrust it to her. That is the best appreciation of her we could show.

Arthur Loesser
Cleveland, Ohio

Contents

1. Teaching—A Creative Art — 1
2. The Modern Approach to Music — 4
3. Basic Principles of Teaching — 9
4. The First Music Lesson — 17
5. Successive Lesson Patterns — 24
6. The First Piano Lesson — 31
7. Personality of the Teacher — 36
8. Understanding the Child — 45
9. The Parent's Role — 50
10. The Adolescent Student — 58
11. The Adult Student — 69
12. The Child Prodigy — 79
13. How to Practice — 89
14. Interpretation — 95
15. Recitals — 100
16. Reconstruction Problems — 105
17. Building a Class — 110
18. Why Pupils Fail — 115
19. Piano Literature — 120
20. Music for the Handicapped — 125
21. Holiday Party — 138

1. Teaching—A Creative Art

> Art is the imposing of a pattern on experience and an esthetic enjoyment in recognition of the pattern.
>
> Alfred North Whitehead

These are provocative words. Are we justified in raising the profession of teaching to the lofty levels of an art? This is not the popular conception. An element of pity often creeps in when it is known that we are merely teachers. The performing artist, on the other hand, has been respected and revered through the ages, and looked upon with a degree of awe. He was considered a being apart from the community in which he lived. In ancient times the inspiration of the music maker was thought to be of divine origin. Primitive tribes placed him close to the chief in authority and importance. Musicians were given a high rank by the Greeks, but it is gratifying to learn of their respect for the profession of teaching and their fostering of what they boldly called an art.

How do we distinguish between artist and teacher? By artist I mean all persons producing fine art—painters, sculptors, poets, musicians, etc. An arresting definition is given of this over-used word. "An artist is one who exhibits art in his work or makes an art of his employment." The popular understanding of a musician as an artist is one who excels in virtuosity, but a wider interpretation is needed.

Further search reveals that the word "create" means to bring into being, to produce, to evolve from one's own thought or imagination. Roget's Thesaurus informs us that to teach is "to instruct, educate, edify, enlighten, inform, guide, direct, infuse, instill, imbue, impregnate, interpret, sharpen the wits, enlarge the mind, open the eyes, bring forward," and, finally, "teach the young idea how to shoot." Does a music teacher dare to take these all-embracing definitions unto himself?

Another important element must be added: the intimate art of communication, on which the basic structure of technique and emotional expression depends. John Donne has said that no man is an island. Matthew Arnold, on the other hand, believed that we were separated by "the salt, estranging sea." Perhaps the truth lies half way between these conflicting conceptions. As we embark upon the vast sea of music, it is the teacher who must use every means in his power to touch, embrace, and understand the future musician entrusted to his care.

The most highly skilled physician cannot hope to communicate with, and ultimately cure, a patient without consideration of the whole man. The source of disease may lie hidden in some underground region of the emotions, far removed from the visible symptoms. Music teachers are not exempt from the need of some knowledge in the special fields of psychology and psychiatry. We have been slow to learn. What musician has not suffered from a teacher so immured in the ivory tower of perfection in his own performance that he totally failed to realize the needs, difficulties, and miseries of the struggling pupil at the piano?

If music is to survive and remain one fixed area of beauty and refuge from the vicissitudes of life in this harassed century, then perhaps as never before, the artist must transmit his art through his pupils. However much may be learned from records left by the masters, it is by personal contact alone that the pupil is shown how the goal was reached.

We cannot view our profession as a trade, a tiresome but necessary means of earning a living. The skill we may have reached in instrumental performance will not enable us to produce in our students a similar result if we ignore the multiple paths leading to artistry. We are working on a broad tapestry with intertwining threads of great complicity.

The final product must have as its base as careful and deliberate a plan as is found in the blueprints of a fine architect. A cathedral does not rise over night. It has existed in the mind of its creator from its inception; countless details were painstakingly planned and difficulties anticipated. So it is with teaching if our goal has height, our understanding depth.

The teacher who is able to make of his profession a creative art in the highest sense, has immeasurably deepened, enriched, and justified his entire existence.

2. The Modern Approach to Music

> All philosophy stands for freeing the school from the idea of instructing the younger generation in that which the older generation held to be science: and in favor of the idea of teaching them what they themselves need. And we see by the history of pedagogic science that every step forward consists in greater natural rapport between pupil and teacher, in less compulsion and greater facilitation of the process of learning.
>
> Thomas Mann

Do you recall your first music lesson?

You were probably placed immediately at the piano and showered with a multiplicity of facts. You were expected to learn simultaneously, the notes on both staffs with treble and bass clefs—time signatures—note values—a new vocabulary of musical terms—and last but not least in difficulty, the manipulation of the piano keys with correct hand position.

The result was often total confusion and unnecessary anxiety. The music of the first melody could not be heard, nor the rhythm felt, since the attention was divided among these many details. You did not see the woods for the trees, nor the trees for the branches.

While the gifted student is able eventually to integrate these conflicting elements, needless time may be consumed; and many students less endowed are lost along the way, their interest killed by such an unpalatable approach. This experience is attested to by many adults who mourn their lost opportunities in the field of music, not realizing that their teachers, not they, should bear the burden of failure.

Alert music teachers, challenged by the task of leading children into the wide province of music, would do well to make a survey of present day methods in other academic fields. They will discover that a revolution has taken place, culminating in what is broadly termed progressive education. From a bewildering number of experiments and theories, ranging from the absurd to the excellent, there emerges a fairly concrete principle. Progressive education is based on the study of the individual child and the freeing of that child from a rigid, unyielding formula of study. This plastic pattern of teaching is molded to the child according to his aptitudes and needs, rather than the child to the pattern. Modern pedagogy cannot truthfully claim this concept to be original as similar theories can be found in the writings of Confucius, Plato, Montaigne, Rousseau, and many others. Each century seems to have produced a few individuals with vision to see the possibilities for good in the liberation of children from the then current system. But in common with all advanced thinkers, these forerunners have always been in the minority.

The study of music seems to have been little affected by progressive principles, judging by the archaic methods still in use by many teachers. Several reasons for this can be found.

1. Music leans heavily upon tradition. Because a music lesson is of an ephemeral nature, few written records have been left. Word of mouth instruction has usually prevailed. Although we find here and there occasional evidences of

inspiring teachers, their disciples have very often transmitted a narrow and sometimes distorted interpretation of the master's theories.

2. Virtuosity has appeared to be the dominating goal, with the merciless demands of technical development taking precedence over the emotional needs of the student.

3. Pupils were given no preliminary training in the fundamentals of music before being taught the piano.

4. Little attention was given to the study of the student's personality. He was not treated as a human being requiring special understanding, but as a receptacle into which music was to be poured, later to ooze from his finger tips. Children with moderate aptitudes, seeking in music a pleasant avocation only, were given especially scanty consideration.

5. The dynamic potentialities of teacher-parent-child relationships have been neglected.

Modern piano pedagogy seeks first to establish a background of musical structure; namely, note learning and singing, the understanding and expression of rhythm through the body before the instrument is approached. The length of time devoted to this early study depends on the age and individual needs of the child or of the adult without previous training. The focal point is music, not the mechanics of the piano. The body is taught to respond to rhythm through such natural media as conducting, clapping, walking, running, etc. The pupil learns to hear, read, and sing simple melodic phrases and to recognize the intervalic relationships involved.

During this period, a constant and searching study is made of each student. A firm and reciprocal friendship should be developed; failing this, no lasting progress can be hoped for.

Since music is fundamentally an art which demands emotional expression, guidance should be sought from those authorities who have made a study of the emotions. Psychologists and psychiatrists have made valuable contributions in this field from which we may benefit. No present day teacher need remain completely in the dark as to the processes of learning—the functioning of the mind and the emotions. Yet music pedagogy and psychology have often remained widely separated subjects.

Perhaps the most significant departure from the old approach lies in the importance of the mother's role as practice helper. She must be made to feel that she is an indispensable partner in the project if the pupil is a child. The dramatis personae of the situation—parent, teacher, and child—are analyzed so that each will know his role. Serious shortcomings in any one member may weaken or wreck the entire structure.

There are many pedagogic paths to be explored. No one so-called "method" can be recommended and followed blindly. We must examine carefully everything available that has a bearing on the subtle art of teaching, boldly discarding that which seems irrelevant. Support for this idea is found in an old saying, "When offered a fish it is not necessary to eat the skin and bones as well as the flesh." Experience alone will give the final answers; it is from our students that we will learn the most.

All phases of modern pedagogy point to the teacher as the catalytic agent who must free and set to work the student's often hidden powers of emotional expression. He must understand and direct the mental processes involved in learning. He must be aware of his own assets and deficiencies and strive to correct the latter. If he is unable through insight and imagination to project himself into the being of the student, he may meet with hostile resistance, and the student remain an unfathomable stranger.

* * *

This book presents a system tested on the piano since the writer is a teacher of piano. But with the exception of the chapters which deal specifically with the beginning lessons, and the literature of the piano, the contents will apply equally well to the teaching of any instrument. Transpose violinist for pianist, and the same ideas fit.

3. Basic Principles of Teaching

> The meaning of education is a leading out, a drawing forth; not an imposition of something on somebody, but an eliciting of what is within him.
> Trench, manure, hoe and water around your young tree, and patiently allow the young fruit to develop of its own juice from the root; your task being as the fruit forms, but to bring in all you can of air and sunshine upon it. It must be coaxed to develop from its individual root.
>
> Sir Arthur Quiller-Couch

Music teachers at the beginning of their careers should abandon the idea that theirs is a specialized art not subject to the rules governing other fields of study. Basic pedagogic procedure is the same in the teaching of language, literature, history, etc. A study of the records left by great instructors of the past will reveal many clues directly and specifically applicable to the teaching of an instrument.

The ultimate goal of every musician is to understand music, and to make music understandingly. This goal must be set before the pupils in turn. By what process can this best be realized? From a wealth of literature available to the inquiring teacher there emerges one recurring theme—the inductive method, which is in essence the drawing out rather than the pouring in of ideas. The individual student is not forced into a rigid plan; instead, the plan is fitted to the needs of the student. This concept is one of the fundamentals of progressive education. Authority for it lies in the writings of inspired teachers, ancient and modern. Various practical concepts emerge from many sources.

1. Proceed from the Known to the Unknown

This principle is emphasized in the teachings of Socrates. A study of the Dialogues of Plato will furnish rich material for investigation by the inquiring teacher. He will find discussions about music which have a startling, modern flavor.

John Amos Comenius in the sixteenth century advised that all instruction be carefully graded and arranged to proceed from the easy to the difficult, the near to the remote, the known to the unknown. He further said that in imparting knowledge to children, the teacher must make constant appeal through sense-perception to the understanding of the child.

These principles should be in operation from the moment the young child enters upon his first music lesson. Specific suggestions will be given in the chapter dealing with The First Lesson, but some modification of this method remains in use throughout the entire period of music study and for students of all ages.

Always use a point of known experience as a bridge to the unknown. Most students are naturally shy, perhaps fearful, in meeting an unknown teacher plus an unknown subject. Self confidence will be greatly strengthened if they are made to realize that they, too, have something to contribute. There are very few children who have not had some experience of music; by skillful questioning they can be led to discuss it and perhaps sing a song learned at school.

Basic Principles of Teaching   11

Teachers of foreign languages use this scheme to make beginning lessons less difficult. The first vocabularies usually consist of words which are similar in sound and spelling to words in the student's native language. Examples:

German	der Mann	the man
	das Haus	the house
French	la table	the table
	la lampe	the lamp

The student is thus beguiled into believing that the formidable new subject is easy. His disillusionment comes when he is better able to accept the real difficulties ahead. So it should be in the teaching of music.

2. Let the Child Discover for Himself

Children love to discover things for themselves. They are happiest when allowed to invent their own games, if imagination has not been dulled and initiative stifled by adult interference. <u>Try to turn every statement of fact into a question whenever possible.</u> This is the direct antithesis of the didactic methods so commonly used in the past. Modern pedagogy encourages constant questions from both teacher and pupil, thus creating a reciprocity of ideas. You will be surprised to discover how few didactic pronouncements are necessary. A child's mind can readily remain inert under the impact of a stated fact, but is stimlated to activity by a direct question.

As early a teacher as Confucius confirms these ideas:

> The superior teacher guides his students but does not pull them along. He urges them to go forward and does not suppress them. He opens the door but does not take them

to the place. Guiding without pulling makes the process of learning gentle, urging without suppressing makes the process of learning easy, and opening the way without leading the students to the place makes them think for themselves.

3. Stimulate the Curiosity

This will follow as a natural sequence if the above principle has been applied. Teachers have no more important function to fulfill than to arouse and keep alive curiosity. Anatole France has said that the whole art of teaching is only the art of awakening natural curiosity. Use "Why?" freely. What happens next? What lies around the corner?

With the introduction of the first folk tunes, interest should be aroused in their titles and the countries from which they originate. "Why are some tunes sad, some gay, some fast, some slow?" Later, as more advanced forms are encountered, "What is a menuet? What kind of a dance? Why the term Sonatina?"

Curiosity about the construction of music should function through each stage of development. Relate the playing of the first chord to the harmonic scheme which will be studied later. Interest in harmony, counterpoint, and musical forms can be created only if the child has been encouraged to be alert as to the structure of the beginning pieces.

4. Principle of Elimination

The study of music offers a labyrinth of paths and we will arrive nowhere if we attempt to follow all at once.

Creative art is both building and throwing away, since its aim is to find an essence. Good teaching can and must fall into this category. In the construction of a sonnet, the limning of an etching, the creating of sculpture—words, lines, or marble must be ruthlessly discarded. On the floor of a sculptor's studio one will often find much waste material—chips of clay, stone or marble. Michelangelo saw in a block of marble the perfect image, later to emerge. His task was merely to set it free from the extraneous substance by means of his chisel and hammer. "The more the marble wastes, the more the statue grows."

Learn to be selective from the first lesson on. Shut off from your mind the multiplicity of facts which must eventually be taught. Choose the most important ones and add to them later. "First things first." Too many new ideas and directions will result in confusion and discouragement for the pupil. The impressions we hope to make must be in a deep groove if they are to be permanent. Avoid verbosity like the plague. Above all, strive for clarity and brevity of expression. A flexible vocabulary is essential. Do not pontificate. Adjust the tempo of learning to the child's capacity, which will vary with the individual.

5. Praise

The teacher who is able to renew with the child his first experiences in music will also be aware of the numerous blocks and checks which stand in the beginner's way. He will therefore be alert to seize opportunities for encouragement as they arise. After curiosity, there is no greater stimulus to learning than praise. But praise is not insincere flattery. It is a reasoned recognition and approval of effort. Avoid exaggerations. Insincerity will be detected and interest killed. The simplest words, such as "Good," "That's better," are sufficient. Do not be afraid to show real enthusiasm if the occasion warrants it. The expression on your face, the tone of your voice, will often communicate your approval; children are more sensitive than adults to these physical signs. If praise is positive in quality and appropriately constant in quantity, your pupil will be better able to accept disciplinary reproof as it becomes necessary. Just praise and fair criticism should counterbalance each other.

No lesson is ever so poor that the child cannot be given one hopeful sign. It may be merely a simple suggestion of your faith in him and his possibilities for betterment. He should never leave with a feeling of complete failure and utter despair. He is too young to bear this burden even though he may be greatly at fault. If we have set a reasonable standard for each child according to his individual capacities, he will know in his heart when he fails to reach it, and unless he is badly spoiled, make a new attempt to improve.

The necessity for praise does not stop with the teaching of children. This is a necessary ingredient for happy results with students of all ages. Each new phase of development presents new difficulties. It is the teacher who must be ever ready to offer understanding encouragement. The adult is sometimes in greater need than the child.

6. Development of the Critical Faculty

Our work is done when the pupil is able to stand alone, though many years must be given to this undertaking. Moral training, which normally begins in the home, must stress the child's ability to make decisions, to judge himself and, as he grows towards maturity, to be independent of parental supervision. A child who has not been given the opportunity to develop these desirable qualities is doomed to failure in later years when all support is withdrawn.

The autocratic attitude of many teachers in former times has been a stultifying influence. A study of the careers of many prominent musicians reveals the crippling effects of too much supervision from both parents and teachers.

The first step towards independence comes when the pupil actually hears what his fingers are playing. He must be guided to listen to himself. I start this activity in the first year at the piano by asking after he has played a little piece, "Was it good? Did you like the way it sounded? Did you make any mistakes?" At first, he may be bewildered and afraid to say that it was either good or bad. He may not even know, in his absorption with the piano keys. By repetition this questioning will bring good results and may become an enjoyable part of each lesson. He is encouraged to continue this activity at home by pretending that he is the teacher and pronouncing judgment on himself. A parent who supervises the practice should be urged to follow this pattern.

The ability to listen is a dominating force in the development of a performing musician. The teacher first sets the standard in his own playing of the student's compositions. As the student progresses he is asked to hear as much fine music as possible and to react frankly; his likes and dislikes should not be frowned upon. The art of criticism demands a slow growth and cannot be superimposed on a young student. Early but indirect guidance will help him to discern the true from the false. The teacher's preferences must be kept in the background, and the teacher himself must finally disappear. It is our lot to be forgotten, a difficult task if our own ego is too demanding. We must be content to live on in our pupils, trusting that the best we have given them will bear fruit.

> It is the custom of schoolmasters to be eternally thundering in our ears as if they were pouring into a funnel and our business is only to repeat what they have said to us. I would have a tutor correct this practice, and at the very outset, according to the capacity of the mind he has to deal with, begin to put it to the test, making it taste things, and by itself choose and discern them, sometimes opening the way to him, and sometimes making him do it for himself. I would not have him think alone and speak, I would have him hear the pupil speak in turn. . . . The fragments borrowed from others he will transform and blend together to make a work that shall be absolutely his own: that is to say, his judgment. His education, labor, and study aim only at forming that.
>
> Montaigne

4. The First Music Lesson

> You know also that the beginning is the most important part of any work, especially in the case of a young and tender thing, for that is the time at which the character is being formed and the desired impression is more readily taken.
>
> Plato
> *The Republic*

The child's first music lesson can be an event of great interest and happiness or it can be a chilling blight. The impressions can be indelible for good or ill. Everything depends upon our ability to incorporate and set in motion the principles of good teaching which will apply to the particular child. We must bear in mind that he is approaching a new subject with emotions which may range from joyful excitement, through passive indifference, to actual fear. At the outset the aim is the creation of a friendly and empathic relationship between teacher and pupil. This is far more important than any musical facts he may learn. There are no set rules as to how contact may be made. A natural, easy manner and simplicity of expression are the key-notes.

Since modern piano pedagogy is based upon a musical foundation which precedes instrumental study, a separate class in the fundamentals of music is highly advisable. In this class, stress would be placed upon singing, notation and reading of music, plus rhythmic expression through the body. However, if such classes are not available, the piano teacher must supply the same instruction. The period of pre-piano study should be extended to at least six months if the child is very young. The piano as such is ignored in this early period.

We may meet with an immediate obstacle—the child's natural eagerness to play the piano and his subsequent disappointment when he finds that this is not our plan. It is imperative that we give as convincing an explanation as possible and try to direct his desire to play into other activities, equally interesting. The mother may need as much persuading as the child.

A practical formula for this necessary substitution might run as follows: "There are many exciting things to learn about music before you play the piano. I am going to teach you to conduct, to clap, to march and to sing. Later, we will learn to read music as you read from a book at school, and when I come to show you how to play the piano, it will be easy, for you will already know a great deal about music."

The first direct approach to music should be made by an endeavor to discover the child's interests. Lead him to talk of his home and school life. Do not persist in questions if he seems shy and reluctant to answer. Direct the conversation towards music. Bear in mind the principle, "Proceed from the known to the unknown." I have never found a child without some previous experience in music. He can usually be stimulated to talk about songs he has heard at school or at home. Ask him to sing one, and accompany him on the piano. If he is slow to do so because of timidity, play or sing for him. But put music of character in the first lesson.

From singing, explore his other possible musical experience such as listening to records, radio, orchestras or bands. Seize upon whatever is offered and use it as a bridge to the unknown. If a band is mentioned, ask, "What instrument keeps the players together?" Many children will have noticed the drum or played upon one. This is our cue for the launching of rhythm, the focal point of the first lesson. Instead of a tedious and confusing definition beyond his understanding, lead him to discover the rhythm that he has unknowingly experienced. The following questions are useful.

"What is there in your body that keeps time and goes on and on?"

Answer: "My heart."

"Have you watched your brother or sister or anyone sleeping? What do they do that also keeps time?"

Answer: "Breathing—sometimes snoring."

"What is there in your house that makes a regular noise over and over?"

Answer: "Clock, vacuum cleaner, egg-beater, etc."

"What other things have you noticed outdoors?"

Answer: "A truck, bus, airplane."

Children with a perceptive, poetic feeling, may mention a variety of natural rhythms such as the rain, the wind, and birds flying. State it simply: "All these things have their own rhythm and all have rhythm." How much better for him to find his own definitions than to have Webster's forced upon him—"Rhythm is a symmetry of movement as determined by recurrent heavy and light accents."

With the aim of correlating rhythmic sense with activities and observations drawn from the child's daily life, ask him to make a list of all the rhythms which he notices during the week, using those mentioned as a starting point. This is his first assignment. Great originality is often displayed as he makes the discovery of rhythm all around him. An interested, observant child will often discover as many as twenty examples. (Be sure the parent does not lend his cooperation in this activity.) We can draw freely upon this list of individually recognized rhythms during future lessons at the piano when a steady rhythm is being emphasized.

The next step after regularity of beat has been demonstrated is the correlating of these notions with the following movements.

1. Clap in march time (2/4 meter). Explain down and up beats. Exaggerate the down beats. Illustrate by dropping a book to the floor. Observe that it is heavy as it falls, light as we lift it up. Ask the child to sit down and stand up as another example of the same feeling. Two/four meter has one heavy, one light beat. These beats are compared to the ticking of a clock or the beat or pulse of the heart.

2. March in two-part time. (The teacher plays a march in simple chordal structure, emphasizing stress of down beat. Avoid harmony or melodic line that will take the attention away from the pulse. A drum is good for this purpose.)

3. Show the child how to conduct in two-part time. Dramatize this activity. The child is the conductor, the teacher the orchestra who plays as the child conducts. The

down-beat starts the music as the baton (pencil) falls, just as the electric light comes on only when we press the switch.

If the child shows good bodily coordination in response to rhythm during clapping, marching, and conducting, we can proceed to three-part meter. Play a short improvisation heavily stressing the down beat.

Ask, "Does the music seem to be heavy, light, or one-two?" Be skillful in drawing out the answer—heavy light, light. Proceed with clapping. Walking in three part meter requires a good sense of balance and should not be pursued if the child seems confused by it. But it is a good test of rhythmic reaction.

Three-part meter is next applied to conducting. The pencil falls on count one, is directed out from the body on count two and up on three, making a triangle. Use the piano to accompany all these activities. Two/four and 3/4 meters are now alternated. Much stress is placed on conducting in the ensuing lessons as most children enjoy it. There is no better way to establish a framework of regular rhythm.

The ear is tested at the conclusion of the first lesson. Play single notes of varying pitches on the piano in different ranges. Ask which tone is high, which low. Next, play a succession of notes in diatonic pattern, working up and down from middle C. The child responds by taking a step forward if the note goes up, and a step backward if the note goes down. Response to pitch will be shown by these simple tests.

A dual process is involved during this extremely important first lesson. The teacher, while making every effort to interest the child and teach him a few basic facts about music, is at the same time attempting some analysis of the child's characteristics.

Four elements are involved:
1. Personality.
    Is he timid, fearful, over-disciplined?
    Is he bold, impudent, over-indulged?
    Is he eager or disinterested?
2. Mental equipment.
    Is his mind slow or quick to grasp new facts?
    What are his reasoning powers?
    Can he concentrate?
3. Musical responses.
    Is he able to carry a tune?
    Can he distinguish a range in pitch?
    Has he perfect pitch?
    Does he react instinctively to rhythm?
    Has he good motor coordination?
    Does he give evidence of any emotional response to music played for him?
4. Physical condition.
    Does he look well?
    Is he unduly nervous or is he lethargic?
    (Later, when he is shown the printed page and the staff, note whether his eyesight is normal. His need for glasses may be discovered at this time.)

It is assumed that the mother is present at all lessons and takes notes on everything that is done. (See chapter on The Parent's Role.)

The above basic outline has been found to be practical with most children. However, it can only be a tentative one, for an unusual reaction in either child or parent may cause us to abandon it completely and seek another approach. We are not omniscient and can hope to glean only a few helpful hints as to the nature and aptitudes of the little stranger. This study must be continued throughout the year.

5. Successive Lesson Patterns

> Keep before you two important principles of education—Timeliness, or giving the student things when he is ready for them; Order, or teaching new facts in proper sequence.
>
> Confucius

The second music lesson should begin with a thorough review of everything presented in the first lesson. Children differ greatly in their powers of assimilation. A gifted child will master quickly the few fundamentals of rhythm which have been taught. On the other hand, if the child is very young, or very slow in learning, it may be necessary to repeat what was previously given, and new ways sought to stimulate his interest. Much depends upon the mother and the kind of support she has given him at home. No specific directions will satisfy the needs of all students. Our own resourcefulness, imagination and elasticity are the guideposts.

The new factor in the second lesson is the introduction of quarter and half notes. They should be referred to by their colors, black and white, not their arithmetical value. A seven-year-old child cannot grasp the multiplication and division involved. Music study should be correlated as much as possible with the first year of school.

1. Ask the child to clap with you a series of quarter notes in a steady rhythmic pattern. Say, "These beats keep

walking. They are black notes when you see them on a page of music." (Show him a staff with notes.) "They are called quarter notes or walking notes." If the unknown word "quarter" is linked with the word "black," a more practical image is presented.

2. Play a chordal pattern of quarter notes and ask him to clap, then walk in time to the music. Develop the idea that the tempo of quarter notes is even, measured, and unhurried.

3. Introduce the staff. Eliminate at first everything but the appearance of the quarter notes in the first piece from the book of folk tunes to be played later.

Ask, "What is their color?" Answer: "Black."

"Quarter notes are black; each one has one count. Find all the quarter notes in this piece. Clap each one."

4. "What is the color of this note?" (pointing to a half note). "This white note is a holding note, a half note. It has two counts. It is twice as long as a quarter note. Clap with me all the half notes holding your hands together as we say one-two."

Next, ask him to guess what kinds of notes you are clapping as you alternate quarters and halves. Be inventive as to devices which will demonstrate these basic note values.

5. Teach him to follow with his feet as he walks, harmonic patterns which you will play using first quarter notes, then halves; then alternate them. If the child finds it difficult to maintain a steady beat in either clapping or walking, give him constant physical aid to avoid discouragement.

6. He should now be ready to return to a more complete study of the staff. Show that the 2 in 2/4 means that there are two counts in a measure.

"What is a measure?" It is the space between the bar

lines. "What is a bar line?" It is like a fence which divides the piece into measures which are like yards. "How many measures in this first piece?" The double bar closes it.

Review all elements learned thus far. Introduce the dotted half note. "This dot, although very tiny, is very powerful. It makes the half note hold one more count." The child should now be reasonably equipped to begin the actual study of the pieces through clapping them in time. Eliminate entirely the reading of the notes unless he already knows them. In this case proceed to Lesson 3.

The Third Lesson is concerned chiefly with the learning of five notes.

Use both staffs, omitting the teaching of the G and F clefs until later.

"A staff has five lines and four spaces." Teach the child to identify each of these five notes by its exact location on a line or space. Use the word "describe" (tell me about). Compare with the description and location of the child's house and street where he lives.

Example: "Middle C is the note with a small line through it. Find all the C's in the first folk tunes."

"What note comes after C?" (D)

"Describe D."
"It is the note just under the first line of the upper staff."
"What note comes after D?" (E). "Describe."
"It is the note on the first line of the upper staff."
Continue in the same pattern with A, B, C on the lower staff. Ask the child to identify these notes wherever they occur in other music shown him. Also, play a game in which you say, "I am thinking of a note that is on the first line of the upper staff," etc. You will know by his answers if he sees the location clearly and is not dependent upon the adjacent ones. This is the quickest way to break down the natural tendency to learn by rote. In turn ask the child to question you in the same way. Encourage the mother to continue this play at home. It may be done away from the piano and can be fun.

Assignment: Repeat this lesson at home each day, with the mother's help, until these five notes are quickly identified and named. They must be recognized wherever they occur. Use extraneous music for this purpose, in order to break down the natural tendency to learn by rote. Each note must be established as a separate entity.

Lesson Four is concerned with singing. When the first five notes can be identified and their exact location described, the child is taught to sing them. At this point you will discover whether or not your pupil has perfect pitch, namely, the ability to identify and sing in correct tonality any note without instrumental aid. While this gift is of great value, much can be done to develop a sense of relative pitch for students who lack this natural ability.

Play middle C. Ask the pupil to match this tone with his voice. Play A, B, C, D, E as he attempts to sing them.

Demonstrate the direction of the voice up, from C to D, and down from C to B. It is often of help to raise the arm as the voice goes up, and lower it as the voice goes down.

One of the advantages of separate theory classes lies in the fact that months can be spent in training the child to sing, not by rote, but by the analysis of whole and half-step relationships. Though the piano teacher cannot devote too much time to this highly important element of music study, he can insist that each tune be sung before it is played. This is a *must* for the entire first year of study. By this method the ear will receive daily training, and the feeling of pitch will be strengthened.

>*Assignment:* Sing each tune, using letter names.
>Sing and conduct each tune.
>Sing and clap each tune.
>Sing and walk each tune.

A basic routine is now established for all subsequent lessons.

Lesson Eight presents eighth notes, which will probably be found in the early folk tunes. Show them to the child. Ask: "How do these black notes differ from the quarter notes that you already know?"

Answer: "They each have a hook or flag."

"They are called running or eighth notes."

Play a pattern of eighth notes on the piano while the child claps in rhythm. Repeat while he runs to the notes played. Be sure that you play nothing but eighth notes. Do not set too fast a tempo.

Clap with him the tunes containing running notes. He is now equipped to recognize and demonstrate walking, holding, and running notes. Make direct application to the next folk tunes.

Teach the new notes which will occur by the same method employed in previous lessons. Use many drills by way of review. Incorporate them into games which will retain the child's interest. Be sure that the first notes learned remain secure as to identity and location.

Two additional meters only will be needed for the first year of study.

4/4: Present this meter in the same manner as 2/4 and 3/4. Omit 6/8 meter until the child is very familiar with the preceding meters.

From now on, try to avoid statements of new things to be learned. Instead, ask questions, encouraging him to apply the knowledge he has already gained. Example: "What does this upper six mean?" (in 6/8). He already knows 2/4 and 3/4. It is now necessary to explain that the lower eight means that an eighth note gets one count. It is like a fast walking note with a separate beat of its own. I like to use the word "magic" at this time. "Eighth notes may no longer run, they must walk." If they each have one count, a quarter note has two, a dotted quarter, three." It is wise to concentrate on 6/8 meter only for two or three weeks as the change in note values is often perplexing to the child.

Two new note values will be needed for the first months of study: the whole note, color white with no stem, occurring in 4/4 meter, and the dotted quarter note. I have found it best to teach this more complicated value in the following way.

[musical notation: 4/4 time, dotted quarter-eighth-dotted quarter-eighth-quarter, counted "1-2 and 3-4 and"]

Walk-dot-run, walk-dot-run. Or, 1-2-and 3-4-and, etc.

Clap these patterns with the child. Keep your hand on his. Be sure he feels the holding power of the dot. Take his hand and step the time values as you walk and count.

The child should by this time have equipment which will enable him to study intelligently simple folk tunes. The length of the weekly assignment can be increased according to his powers of assimilation. Allow much time for review. Be prepared to repeat many times if necessary all preceding routines. Make sure the foundation is secure before the instrument is attempted.

6. The First Piano Lesson

> The lyf so short,
> The craft so long to lerne,
> Th'assay so hard, so sharp
>   the conquering.
>
> Chaucer

There is no more important event than the first piano lesson. It should not be given until the elements of rhythm, note learning and singing as presented in the previous lessons have been mastered. The child may become restive during the last weeks of pre-piano study and frequent mention should be made of the fact that the long anticipated day is drawing close. When it arrives we must share with him the pleasure and excitement in the exploration of the piano.

The color and grouping of the piano keys should first be studied before any attempt is made to play them. Use as few statements and ask as many questions as possible.

"What color are the keys?"

"How are the black keys arranged?" (By twos and threes.)

"Middle C is always at the left of the two black keys in the middle of the piano. It is the same C that you know on the staff. Before every two black keys you will always find a C."

"Find all the C's on the piano."

"What note lies between two black keys?" (D)
"Find all the D's."

Continue this pattern to include five notes: A, B, C, D, E. These notes must be securely located on the piano just as they were on the staff. They will be the first ones used in the beginning folk tunes played. The correlation of the note to be read on the staff with the key of the piano must be established without benefit of rote learning—namely, depending on the adjacent key for identification. Use many drills until you are sure the child recognizes each key by itself. The lack of this early discipline is often the dominating cause of poor sight reading.

The dramatic moment for the actual playing of the piano has now arrived. Be sure the bench or chair is of the right height. This is determined by the size of the child. He must neither perch on too high a bench, nor sit so low that his wrists drag downwards. His posture should be as upright as possible, but not fixed or rigid. The body must be free to move; lean slightly towards instead of away from the piano. Do not lean against the back of the chair; this will throw the body weight backwards, away from the field of action. A footstool is advisable for very small children so that their legs do not dangle in mid-air. Adjust the music rack to the individual; discover what distance affords him the clearest vision.

Eliminate all but the fewest necessary factors for playing.

1. Let the arm hang at the side. It should feel relaxed and heavy. The best means for reducing arm tension, which usually occurs at this point, lies not in words but in actually taking hold of the pupil's arm. Pull down gently on the elbow, which is apt to be held too high; press lightly on the muscles of the forearm. If the tension is extreme,

ask the pupil to stand up and swing his entire arm back and forth with a free motion of the shoulder.

2. Make a fist of the hand. Open the fingers and place them on the piano in a somewhat curved position, as if the hand were holding a ball. The thumb rests on middle C.

Separate Hands:

[musical notation]

3. Play the above exercises for two octaves up from middle C with the right hand, and down from middle C with the left hand; count two on each note. (This will hold the child to a slow tempo which is most essential.) Demonstrate the pattern, calling attention to the skip between the thumb and second finger. Ignore hand position and names of notes for this first attempt.

4. For the second playing of the exercise, curve and lift each finger very slightly, up and back, before it strikes the key. This is the beginning of finger independence. The action of the fingers must be isolated, one from the other. The tone should be light, as the muscles are as yet untrained and weak. Too loud a tone indicates arm pressure which we do not want. Each key must be held down until the next one is struck and then released. This is usually difficult, for the fingers may have a tendency to overlap instead of making a quick release. It is helpful to compare the action of the fingers with the feet in walking. One foot lifts up as

the other comes down. Walk with the child and encourage him to observe what his feet are doing. Then try to transfer the same physical movement to the fingers. This is the first lesson in legato playing. Correlate with speech or singing in which words or tones are not run together; neither are they completely separated.

5. Keep the arm relaxed and fairly low in position, the wrist as flexible as possible. It should be thought of as a hinge which is free to move in any direction as needed. The arch of the hand should not cave in. Instead, the knuckles must be reasonably prominent. Use an architectural principle in explanation. A curving or arched dome gives the greatest support to a cathedral or auditorium. Later, when the hand is required to play heavy chordal structures, greater power is obtained by a high rather than a low arch.

It is impossible for any beginner to grasp and put in action all these basic directions in an early attempt at playing. The plastic molding of the hand to the piano is a continuous process. It is greatly facilitated by the teacher's own hand on the pupil's, helping it to assume the correct position and reducing tension in the wrist and arm. Instructors in the dance often use this principle when, instead of words, they place a refractory arm or leg in the way it should go. A stern command to "relax" is usually followed by greater muscle strain.

The first folk tunes which the child has studied previously are now to be played. If the notes were securely learned through singing, time values understood through walking and clapping, the transition from the staff to the piano is not difficult. Letter names should be sung as the notes are played to maintain complete accuracy of note placement. This is the rule for all successive lessons. Each tune must be clapped, walked, and sung before it is played. Counting while playing should be deferred until definite proof has been given that notes are instantly recognized as the piano key is struck.

The child's delight in his first experience at the piano is greatly enhanced if the teacher provides a simple harmonic base to his first attempt. He will have the illusion that he is really making music and, better still, it seems so easy. Unless the child is exceptionally talented, the first assignment should consist of not more than three or four pieces.

7. Personality of the Teacher

> . . . our ideal teacher will need the second qualification of an already accumulated wealth. These hungry pupils are drawing all their nourishment from us, and have we got it to give? They will be poor, if we are poor; rich if we are wealthy. We are their source of supply. Every time we cut ourselves off from nutrition, we enfeeble them. And how frequently devoted teachers make this mistake! dedicating themselves so to the immediate needs of those about them that they themselves grow thinner each year. We all know the "teacher's face." It is meagre, worn, sacrificial, anxious, powerless. That is exactly the opposite of what it should be. The teacher should be the big bounteous being of the community.
>
> George Herbert Palmer

Teachers would do well to turn a searching light inward at the outset of their careers and evaluate their strength, weakness and aptitude for the task ahead. It need hardly be pointed out that anyone lacking a genuine fondness for children is not fitted to teach them anything. Taking this premise for granted, what further characteristics are essential to the successful teacher?

He must, first of all, possess some degree of insight and imagination. Only through their functioning can he be aware of the child's reactions—his joys and fears. The adult must be able to reproduce within himself the same perplexities which assail the young student. His own mastery of the subject at hand must be forgotten temporarily, and he should strive to understand how it appears to the uninitiated. The bond of sympathy essential to the full development of the child's musical abilities cannot be established without the use of imagination. The technical term, empathy, in current use by psychologists, has a special significance for anyone in the teaching profession. Empathy is a mental entering into the feeling or spirit of a person. It induces in us an appreciative perception or understanding. We may suffer with another when we offer sympathy, but with empathy we are no longer an outsider —our imagination enables us to feel how the problem is from the inside.

Enthusiasm is also a primary requisite for the successful teacher. He should consider teaching a privilege rather than a necessity. This is possible only if he views it in the light of a creative art, no less important than his own personal attainments as a pianist. The quality of virtuosity is rare. The musician who has this gift must of necessity bow to its demands. But such a person may never fulfill himself as a teacher since his need to perform must take precedence over all other desires. There remains, however, the large majority of musicians who find in teaching a means of continuing the development of their talent through their pupils. Enthusiasm is nourished as they observe the successful results of their efforts. In among the succeeding classes of varying degrees of aptitude there may be one child with the mark of true, even of great, talent. It is the rare and greatly to be pitied teacher who does not rise to this challenge and whose zest for teaching is not increased accordingly.

It is an unfortunate tendency for some teachers to look

upon teaching as a necessary but unpleasant drudgery—a sort of musical salt mine. These aspirants consider a playing career of paramount importance and begrudge the time and effort that must be spent on their pupils. This attitude can hardly be concealed. There is no surer way to kill a perceptive child's awakening interest than to let him know by indirection of your lack of interest.

Should the earnest teacher abandon his goal as a pianist and conscientiously devote all his time and creative energy to his pupils? No. To combine performance with instruction is a challenge which requires both effort and common sense. Still, brilliant records in all the many artistic disciplines are conclusive evidence that it can be done. Physicians have managed similarly to co-ordinate the practice of medicine with teaching, and in science the combination of research with pedagogy is not the exception, but the rule. Countless writers and artists who are obliged to teach long hours, have nevertheless proved their ability to produce their own work.

The piano teacher can do the same if he is convinced of the necessity and the desirability of playing a double role. Then also, he must be skillful in proportioning his time. This calls for a constant self-discipline which will enable him to vary the balance between the two forms of endeavor as the situation changes, while maintaining a reasoned equilibrium. Teaching and playing must nourish each other. The teacher who cuts out for himself time for his own practice will thus enrich his aspirations for performance. In so doing he will increase the store from which he gives to his pupils.

Teaching is in essence an expenditure of knowledge scaled with enthusiasm. No teacher can maintain his store of interest-energy if he does not replenish it frequently and with just as much purpose as he does his bank account. The teacher's period of daily practice will retain both skill and interest. It will enable him to play for his pupils as occasion arises. Sacrifice of the practice hours will so diminish the teacher's resources that he himself may lose interest and the pupil will unfailingly recognize the fact.

The teacher's enthusiasm for the project in hand is first conveyed to the child through the channel of simple friendliness. The adult with a demonstrative personality has therein a great natural advantage. However, it is not an insurmountable obstacle to be timid and retiring. The first step is to recognize these qualities for what they are. If you find so much difficulty in meeting new people and new situations as to hinder you in your work, consultations with a thoroughly grounded psychologist or psychiatrist may be in order. But do not expect a new personality as you might new clothing. At the best, you will find only a better self-appraisal and a new and more confident technique in handling yourself. And it will take time.

It is not easy for an inexperienced teacher to make the transition from being the recipient of knowledge to that of the giver. Remember that the child may be struggling with his own insecurity and yours must be concealed from him. You as the leader must turn his fears into confidence. Assume authority though you may not feel it, and with successive attempts you will find a genuine quality replacing your earlier artifices.

One of the greatest assets a teacher can possess is a sense of humor. Little advice can be offered as to its nurture, though much has been written about this hard-to-define and elusive trait. Its acquisition by those so unfortunate as to be born lacking this desirable quality is doubtful. But if humor is present in even the slightest form, its appropriate use is strongly urged. Emerson advises teachers to smuggle in a little contraband wit. Nothing is more deadly or more resented by a child than a forced humor. If you will permit yourself an easy naturalness of expression such as you would use with your contemporaries, you will find the child quick to respond. Lightness of touch is everything. The most weighty and difficult problems can be immeasurably eased by a humorous rather than a ponderous approach. The heavy-handed attitude of a teacher who views his profession with too great a solemnity will dampen and chill all the natural gaiety of children. But the child, given a chance, can often initiate the unskilled adult into a long-forgotten world of fancy.

Just as elasticity is required in the handling of the teacher's personal problem of combining instruction with his own performance, this quality is equally necessary in the teaching of children. The rigid, unbending teacher, fixed on one way of approach only, is due for a rude surprise. He will be dismayed to discover that his carefully thought out plan does not work with every child. Rather, he must be flexible and quickly adopt new methods of procedure as the pupil's needs suggest. Such resourcefulness and the ability to abandon one mode and substitute another when the occasion demands, are a real necessity. Many teachers may find this difficult because they think in terms of their own perhaps severe and inelastic training. It may seem an insurmountable task to rid oneself of a residual inflexibility. It can be done only if the fault is recognized, squarely faced, and deliberately worked on.

We must strive unendingly for the quality of patience.

A slow-thinking, slow-moving child becomes confused and miserable, his processes of learning retarded even more, by a quick-moving impatient teacher personally unable, but seemingly unwilling, to comprehend a personality so different from his own. If these are your characteristics, seek to develop the art of relaxation. Sit back in your chair. Speak gently. Move quietly. Avoid sharp commands. Search for new ways of repeating the same directions without irritability. Search perhaps for your own peace of mind, and if it cannot be found easily, search for the things that have disturbed it and set you back on yourself.

The choice of words used in teaching a child is highly important. They should be determined by the vocabulary of the student, but the teacher must not be afraid of enlarging that vocabulary. Children are attracted by an occasional word that is new to them. While sparing use should be made of pedantic definitions, nothing is more deplorable than to talk down to a child in a form of pseudo baby-talk. He will be far happier in hearing words and expressions which are sometimes above his understanding than those which aim beneath it.

If you are inclined to sarcasm, abandon any trace of it when dealing with a child. It is a childish weapon at best, of doubtful good for any age, carrying with it great potentialities for cruelty. By the same token never laugh at a child, only with him, no matter how ludicrous his remarks or reactions may be. Nothing will drive him further from you, or set up a greater barrier. This statement will doubtless be verified by your own childhood experiences. There is probably no adult who does not bear the mark of having been ridiculed at a tender age. This is a potent and far-reaching factor in creating timidity and insecurity, and will set to naught the teacher's other efforts and abilities.

Any analysis of the teacher's personality would be incomplete without some mention of physical characteristics since the child's first impressions come through his eye and ear. Children are more aware than adults realize of how things and people look. They love colors, and if their teacher is a woman they enjoy seeing her in bright, attractive dresses. Who does not remember the dreary school teacher who wore the same brown dress week after week? More important than the clothes you wear is the expression of your face, your smile, your eyes, your gestures, the tone of your voice. If you are the unfortunate possessor of a harsh, strident voice, go to any lengths to remedy it, even if it necessitates a course in speech correction. Since speech is the chief medium by which the teacher's thoughts are transmitted to the student, too much stress cannot be placed on the quality as well as the manner of the spoken word. A wavering and over-gentle voice will not command attention or respect. Some voices ask to be ignored by their pleading ineffectualness.

Every teacher by virtue of the demands upon him must find ways to keep his enthusiasms alive, and to enlarge his store of knowledge. The richness or paucity of his background will be revealed to the student through the weekly lessons. If the teacher as well as the pupil is to grow, nourishment must be sought not only from his own study and performance as a pianist, but through literature and the allied arts. The deep but narrow channel of a musical education too often excludes the study of many subjects which can be explored with pleasure and profit throughout the years of teaching. The mature musician who has kept his own curiosity alive will be interested to examine contemporary music. He will not be content to lean only upon the traditions of the past, but will have an open mind for each modern facet of development. The failure of a career can often be traced to the lack of this life-giving attribute. The combined professions of teaching and performance can be greatly enriched and nourished by an ever-widening store of interests.

One question remains to be asked: Do we find joy in teaching and do we impart that joy? If we look upon our daily lessons as a dreary grind and resent the sacrifice of our own practice, our students are sure to react in kind. G. H. Palmer has said: "Harvard College pays me for doing what I would gladly pay it for allowing me to do. Our goal should be to increase the social service of our teaching and to perfect joy in our work."

The elusive quality of happiness is not easily obtained, nor is it humanly possible to project a joyous feeling at all times. We can, however, keep the desirability of this emotion in sight and be careful to conceal the opposite qualities of gloom and heaviness of spirit which are sure to attack us at times.

Our efforts must be doubled for the inhibited, timid child who needs the constant encouragement which will be evident in our attitudes. If we are tense—and tension is an ever-present enemy in our so-called Age of Anxiety —the feeling of hurry, of trying to keep up with the clock will militate against serenity. Teachers, of all people, must at any cost keep their own inner perturbations hidden.

The various elements of personality discussed in this chapter are of vital importance, but no teacher can be expected to possess them all. Starting with his native endowment he can strive to supplement and develop what he is lacking. The first step comes with the realization that only through the warmth and vitality of his own nature can he hope to win the elusive student who looks to him for guidance and inspiration.

8. Understanding the Child

> Know you what it is to be a child? It is to be something very different from the man of today. It is to have a spirit yet streaming from the waters of baptism, it is to believe in love, to believe in loveliness, to believe in belief; it is to be so little that the elves can reach to whisper in your ears; it is to turn pumpkins into coaches, and mice into horses, lowness into loftiness and nothing into everything, for each child has its fairy godmother in its soul; it is to live in a nutshell and to count yourself the king of infinite space. . . . Children's griefs are little, certainly, but so is the child, so is its endurance, so is its field of vision, while its nervous impressionability is keener than ours.
>
> Francis Thompson

The relationship between teacher and child may be the closest tie outside the family circle. This can only be established if we are able to enter his world. We cannot expect him to enter ours. It is impossible to read what goes on behind the seemingly clear and open-eyed gaze of a child. Be sure he is measuring us at our first meeting, and making judgments accordingly. Our superiority of age and knowledge must be discarded if we are ever to fathom his inscrutable little personality. The memories of our own childhood may be an aid if we can recall the varying emotions with which we approached music study. We must see with his eyes, hear with his ears, react with him to each new impression as if we too were receiving it for the first time. It is possible to rediscover the pleasure in singing, the exciting rhythmic pulse in music, the stress of the down beat, the staff with its confusing lines and spaces, and the mysterious black and white keys of the piano which will produce the first melody.

We are a stranger to him, as he is to us, and whatever his external attitude may be, at heart he desires our approval. If we can find the intuitive skill to offer him simple friendship immediately, a bridge leading to the deeper qualities of trust and affection may be built.

The child's identification with his teacher is a vital factor in what he will be able to produce in any creative art. This powerful incentive to learning must be recognized as the lever which moves mountains. Too many children have been the victims of unimaginative teachers who through inhibitions of their own, or lack of empathy, considered it beneath them to offer and win affection, and to whom a warm, personal relationship was to be avoided. Neither is it right to look down upon a child as from a great height. A reasonable level can be found without loss of respect. A child does not "take a lesson" as if in spite of the teacher. This outmoded expression is indicative of the evil embodied in this attitude. Instead of "taking" he should be encouraged to give and share in the mutual exploration of music.

The study of any child offers a richer field to the perceptive teacher than any book of pedagogy ever written. Endless dissimilarities will be found since no two children will exhibit identical characteristics. Awareness is the essential quality if we have any hope of learning about the child at the piano. We can quickly discover from his response to our initial inquiries if he is fearful, interested, happy, or not. A lesson need never be considered wasted if a con-

Understanding the Child 47

fidence is offered about his daily life—topics which would seem to have no bearing on the subject of music, but which may furnish valuable clues and throw new light on his unknown personality. If, on the other hand, he is apparently uninterested, silent and unresponsive, we must try a different approach, abandon questions, and converse on perhaps trivial subjects which may put him more at ease. We must not be disturbed at his seeming withdrawal, but instead seek to discover the causes.

A poignant memory comes to mind, illustrative of this situation. A small boy who had always prepared excellent lessons and with whom I had thought a firm friendship was established, was completely uncommunicative and silent at one lesson. He had obviously done no practicing whatsoever. After too many questions on my part as to why and wherefore, he suddenly burst into tears and said, between his sobs, "My dog died." I learned the hard way—a lesson I have never forgotten.

Most children respond to affection, but unfortunately there are some whose home life is unhappy and who have come to view all adults, especially those in authority, with suspicion. Any child must be considered not merely as a piano student, but as a product of his home and school environment. Some factor in these, if overlooked, can result in failure in music. Emotional disturbances must be recognized and their cause and remedy sought. This is a very delicate area requiring much tact on the part of the teacher. Many parents resent any interference in the realm of parental authority which might tend to point a finger at their own lacks.

Thomas Wolfe considered the relation of a fine teacher to a student to be just below the relation of a mother to her son. There are mothers who oppose a growth of intimacy with anyone else and may complain that the child does not confide in them as he does in his teacher. The maternal instinct is a powerful one. We must be careful to avoid any seeming usurpation of the mother's role in the child's life and set definite boundaries as to the limits of our own influence. If we do not, we stand to lose a pupil. We must, however, have the courage to recommend professional aid should the child's problems of adjustment seem extreme. It is impossible to detach his inner anxieties from the study of the piano. We will reach an impasse if this is not recognized. Everything depends upon the initial relationship between parent, teacher, and child. If this is at fault, our advice will not be welcome. We can increase our own understanding by a study at times of the literature offered by Child Guidance Clinics and parents' magazines. Trends in child psychology are changing so rapidly that we must strive to keep abreast.

There are some young teachers who approach children with apprehension since their own experience has been devoid of any contact with them. I urge such a person to cultivate children of all ages, wherever they can find them, to observe their play, their games, their jokes, and then endeavor to participate in them. Find out what children like to read and why. It is most enlightening to read their literature, especially poetry written for and about children. Often it is the poet who is closest to the child's heart and imagination. We can learn from him. I often ask children to write little stories about the early folk tunes they are playing which have descriptive titles. This calls forth the use of their own imagination. These stories in which they usually delight are never duplicated, for every reaction will be different and may reveal to us something of his inner life.

Complete understanding of any human being, adult or child, is an unattainable goal. The best-intentioned teacher in the world cannot hope to solve a problem that has vexed poets and philosophers through the ages. He can, as his perceptiveness increases through experience and study, discover new ways to decrease the distance between the pupil and himself. This is his ever present responsibility.

9. The Parent's Role

> Would a musician let a pupil make a wild attack on the keyboard or invent intervals to please himself? No, the striking thing is that nothing is left to the choice of the learner. The element in which he is to work is fixed, the tool he must use put into his hands, even the way he must use it is prescribed—I mean the change of fingers in order that one get out of the other's way and make the path plain for its successor; until by dint of this regulated cooperation and thus alone, the impossible becomes possible.
>
> Goethe

Regulated cooperation, which Goethe advises in the above quotation, is directly applicable to the role the parent must play in the study of the piano. No young child can be expected to fulfill all that the teacher has set forth for practice without daily adult aid. The progress of the student is a direct reflection of the help and intelligence of the parent. The interrelationship of teacher, parent, and child can be compared to a musical triad in which the combination of intervals produces the chord. The absence of any one part creates a failure in the whole.

The growth of Parent-Teacher Associations in all fields of education gives evidence of the great need for cooperation between parents and teachers. The study of music must follow suit. Most parents who see the fine results of their conscientious labor are convinced of its necessity. The reluctant ones can be persuaded to cooperate if we as teachers set forth our ideas with tactful understanding of the mother's busy schedule. The first interview is our opportunity to explain fully the complexities of the new venture and to state boldly that success or failure depends upon the mother's willingness to work with us.

A convincing approach is the comparison of piano study with the subjects taught in school where the mind is focused upon one set of facts only, as in reading, writing, and arithmetic. The piano demands coordination of numerous elements which must be grasped immediately, since the student must recognize instantly the notes on the staff and at the same time locate them on the piano. He must use the right fingers, observe the proper time values and maintain correct hand position. The preliminary study of theory, namely, rhythmic response and note learning through singing, simplifies but does not entirely solve the difficulties. It is the adult mind which must give the proper guidance to the frequently bewildered child.

Weekly contact with the teacher usually consists of a thirty minute lesson. What is a seven-year-old child to do in the remaining six days if left completely to his own resources? He is sure to need an adult by his side whether he is gifted or has only a modicum of talent. Remind the parent that in school the teacher is present the entire day to offer guidance or administer discipline.

The study of the piano can be a solitary and discouraging pursuit to a child who is left to flounder alone in the unknown sea of music. I have seen many such children approach the piano with enthusiasm only to lose interest rapidly and eventually abandon the undertaking if the mother is absent. The cause was not hard to find. They lacked the maturity for self-guidance.

No child can be expected to assimilate all the factors involved and to practice painstakingly by himself. He will usually stumble through the lesson unaware of errors. By the time a week has passed he will have practiced his mistakes so thoroughly that they may well be ineradicable. The greatest practical aid a parent can give is to prevent and correct mistakes.

There is, however, a deeper and more poignant need for the mother's presence. She will be able to share in the pursuit of an art which may provide pleasure throughout the student's life whether or not he becomes a professional musician.

The most frequent objection is made by the parent who has had no musical training herself and is appalled by the idea that she must be a guide. I assure such a mother that she need not play the piano but if she is present at all lessons, a silent listener, taking notes on all that is said and done, she will be able to set up a miniature daily lesson at home. Her adult mind will quickly grasp the simple steps which are geared to the understanding of a young child.

I often cite the example of the parent of one of my most gifted pupils. The mother was dismayed when I explained the role I wished her to play. She tearfully confessed that music study had been denied her and that she was not competent to help her child. It was only after considerable urging that she consented to make the attempt. The result was outstandingly successful. She was able to give the most expert supervision in a relatively short time and this activity became a most joyful experience. Long after this child ceased to need her assistance the mother asked permission to come to the lessons for she found great pleasure in being an appreciative audience of one. This woman became through the years an acute critic of musical performances; her horizons were widened and now she takes an active part in local music education in many fields. I must add that this mother's personality was such that she never intruded on the teacher-child relationship and in later years was happy to watch the exciting development of her child's professional career without interference but with intelligent understanding.

The happy example just cited is unfortunately not always typical of what we may expect. I audit hundreds of children each year attempting to evaluate their abilities and needs and to select the proper teacher. I am aware in the first few moments of the interview of some of the obvious difficulties. There are as many types of parents as there are children. Today we hear much of the permissive method of child training. This theory, if carried too far, results in a totally undisciplined child. Such a one may wander about the room, interrupting the conversation without remonstrance from the mother. It is apparent that parental control is lacking and it is doubtful that his mother will be able to direct the child's music practice with any degree of authority. Such a situation presents one of our most difficult problems. I do not, however, consider it a hopeless one. An intelligent parent, if carefully advised by an experienced teacher, may come to see his indulged child in a different light and take gradual steps to correct the situation. I cannot too greatly stress the need of such an interview before music lessons have begun. I have known teachers who, after months of lessons, have never even met the mother. Pupils were deposited at their door and called for later. Their lack of success was inevitable.

What of the mother who is overly eager to participate in the lessons? She may answer all the questions addressed to the child, thus demonstrating her own aggressive ambitions. Her child is usually repressed and silent and constantly glances in the mother's direction. It is impossible to make a happy contact with the child under such circumstances and I take time for a few moments to talk with the mother alone after the lesson. I urge her to take no active part while I am teaching the child and explain the reasons as tactfully as possible, suggesting that instead she take notes on all that is said and done. It is wise to place such a mother at a distance from the piano, preferably behind the pupil where she cannot be seen. I try in succeeding lessons to handle this touchy problem with as light a touch as possible saying to the child, "Let's pretend that your mother is the wall paper. I won't talk to her but only to you and she will not say a word to us." Naturally I am hoping that the parent will take this dual admonition to herself. It must be admitted that there are extreme situations where our words fall on stony ground and the mother remains fixed in her rigid pattern of interference. If such is the case and all attempted persuasions have failed it may be necessary to ask that she not come to the lesson. Unless this child is unusually intelligent and has shown some degree of self-discipline, we cannot hope for much progress.

Other mothers unconsciously transmit their own fears and insecurities to the child, who will demonstrate anxiety —fear of the unknown and lack of confidence. He is terrified that he may make a mistake and finds it almost impossible to answer questions lest he say the wrong thing.

I sometimes see such a mother literally wringing her hands as her child is attempting to play. She too lives in terror of mistakes.

These are only a few of the dilemmas which face teachers. How can we hope to change the personality of an adult, especially if we are young and inexperienced? How far can we intrude upon the fixed patterns of family life? How can we establish discipline in the child if the mother cannot? How can we build self-confidence if the mother is overpowering? We must assume that even the most misguided mother has the best interest of her child at heart. I have seen situations which seemed hopeless at first gradually improve under the firm but kindly treatment given by the teacher.

How can time and opportunity be found to acquaint parents with their musical responsibilities since private lessons are usually confined to half an hour? In addition to the suggestions previously made as to the discussion in the first interview, I have found it very helpful to have a small social hour for parents at intervals during the year. Many problems can be discussed over a cup of tea. In the case of a recalcitrant mother much can be said objectively to a group that could not be said to the individual. Mothers should be encouraged to present their problems at such a gathering and the questions raised are often common to the group. It takes only one or two intelligent and co-operative women to start the conversation. Skillful leading on the part of the teacher can focus attention on practice routines (how much time each day, what part of the day is best), and most important, how the mother can give musical guidance. It is not unusual to hear a grievance aired which can be answered by others rather than by the teacher. These mothers for the most part are familiar with similar discussions in their P.T.A. groups in public schools and often find it stimulating and a helpful experience to find the same approach in the field of music.

I have so far emphasized the role of the mother. In some cases it may be the father or an older child who must assume responsibility for the child's piano study. The same procedures should be presented. As the child's self-criticism develops in his practice he will become more and more capable of working without supervision. It is wise to emphasize this theory from the very first lesson for the mother may be relieved to know that hers is not a life sentence.

I begin building independence, after a few months of study, by assigning the pupil one or two pieces to prepare unaided. This serves as a test of his reliability. The weaning should be a gradual but steady process. Little by little the mother will be able to withdraw, and the happy day will arrive when the student can be trusted to work by himself. The presence of two adults in the room is a mixed blessing, for the teacher can only come to an intimate understanding of his pupil when they are alone together. It is a good idea to ask the mother to absent herself occasionally. In a week of absence a note to her will apprise her of the next assignment.

The Parents Council of The Cleveland Institute of Music has developed a very interesting Family Night, which is eagerly anticipated each year. This program presents both parents and children. A teacher may discover by questioning that one or the other parent has at some time played or sung even though in the distant past. Many a father has been persuaded (though I admit with some coaxing) to take down his trumpet or clarinet from the attic where it has lain forgotten for several years and practice up for the big night accompanied by his child. A mother who has studied singing in former years may sing a simple folk song with the young pianist at the piano. An enterprising teacher can, without too much difficulty, make an arrangement for such family recitals. There have been some surprising combinations at these programs. It is not unusual for a family of three, four, or five to perform together. We have had among other instruments violin, flute, clarinet, drums, horn, guitar, voice, and of course the piano, often for four hands.

A young teacher starting a class can find no better way of legitimately advertising what he has to offer. The social aspects of such an event create an intimacy which is invaluable. New friendships are often formed, for these parents have a common bond, the musical training of their children.

It is a hard task for an inexperienced teacher to assume the role of mentor and advisor to the adult parent who may be resentful of his demands. Success can come if he himself is convinced of the necessity of parent aid. He will find individual ways of transmitting his enthusiasm and eliciting the needed support. The good results obtained will offer lasting proof as to the validity of his ideas.

10. The Adolescent Student

> All the time I am talking, I am talking to you
> Trying to make it true,
> I am trying to say, Be sure,
> Endure. It will be the way you want it.
> I am remembering when I was wild, too,
> Secret. Rich. Unknown
> Except to one friend. Even then alone.
> I am asking what you want to be,
> Asking what you want of me,
> Telling you there is nothing in yourself
> Ever to fear.
> And wondering if you hear.
>
> John Holmes

Today's press offers alarming evidence of adolescent delinquency. Many hard beset parents and teachers may agree secretly with Shakespeare when he writes, "I would there were no age between ten, and three and twenty, or that youth would sleep out the rest."

What shall our procedure be when a formerly docile and interested piano student appears to undergo a metamorphosis before our very eyes? Suddenly he presents a problem which taxes all our powers of ingenuity: how to keep him on the musical path for which he has demonstrated a predilection.

Adolescence is a transition period from childhood to adulthood. It is an uncharted territory where dangers threaten on all sides. It is a no-man's land through which every young person must pass. He has no way of understanding either the physical changes or the turbulent emotions which are disturbing him. Since his natural state may be one of defiance, it is easy for him to become a prey to the attractions of delinquency with its flaunting of authority.

Juvenile courts give ample proof that punishment is not the only solution to many misdemeanors for which youth is arraigned. The cause may lie concealed in the early years of childhood when idleness and lack of direction provide a rich soil for later disintegration. There are some children who seem able to accept the burden of adolescence gracefully and without undue pain to themselves, their parents and teachers. There are many more who suffer real confusion and unhappiness.

Signs of adolescence can appear as early as the age of ten and as late as seventeen. The discerning adult cannot wait for physical signs but will be on the alert for emotional forerunners. The hitherto happy, alert, well-adjusted child who becomes tearful, irritable, careless, lazy, indifferent, moody, is suspect. Teachers are sometimes more aware of personality changes than parents who are with their children constantly, just as physical changes are more apparent in persons whom one sees infrequently. Many parents are at their wits' end, unable to comprehend what has happened to their sunny, agreeable child. They are often appalled and unwilling to admit that the cause is a simple (or not so simple) case of adolescence.

The key to the sympathetic understanding of the loneliness and insecurity of adolescence lies in the adult's ability to recall his own emotions during this period. This is far more difficult than reliving the happier experiences of childhood since it is a normal instinct to obliterate what is unpleasant. These disturbed years are often consigned to limbo through a self-protective "will to forget." The exploration of these submerged memories will greatly increase the adult's sensitivity to the adolescent's problems. It should enable him to offer guidance which perhaps he was denied.

Music may be the saving element for a young person floundering in the bewildering bog of adolescence. A child who has shown an early interest in music and for whom regular practice is a daily activity has a valuable fortification. The piano can be a tool of great therapeutic value if we as teachers have the wisdom to use it wisely.

A sound personal relationship between teacher and pupil founded on mutual respect and regard is essential. The piano teacher who is emotionally secure himself may serve as a pattern for the development of the pupil's own powers of self-discipline. This is the age of hero worship and "crushes," which should be accepted without condemnation or comment. Much good can be obtained from the desire for identification with the teacher. The responsibility imposed on us is often very heavy. We have a dual task—to offer and accept friendship and at the same time make sure that healthy limits are maintained.

The adolescent is apt to express his difficulties in a mixture of two conflicting moods—rebellion and dependence. He longs to escape parental authority and at the same time needs protection and guidance, which he finds difficult to accept from his own family. Thus he may seek assistance from some mature person outside the family circle. The music teacher in whom he has confidence and regard may be the natural choice.

Authorities who have made a searching study of adolescence agree that this phase is characterized by passivity, restlessness, loss of interest, desire for isolation, day-dreaming, neglect of work, instability, loss of skill in performance, and withdrawal from parents, teachers, and friends. However, there are some young people who feel a great need for ganging together with their contemporaries. This is the age for secret societies, for eccentricities in dress, manners, and speech. Rebellion against organized study, the piano in particular, may be a symbol of the child's revolt against parental authority if the parent has shown too intense a demand for progress. The adolescent may reject the very thing he most desires in the attempt to express his burgeoning adulthood.

Faced with these formidable reactions, what is the piano teacher to do? The student must be persuaded at a very early stage to look upon his teacher as a friend, not a foe. This is not an easy task, for the very fact that the teacher is an adult automatically raises a barrier of age. A meeting ground may be found if we are able to convey without too many words our sympathetic understanding. The ever present goal should be the development of self-reliance in the student, but it must be remembered that the ability to stand alone comes by gradual degrees. Many regressions and failures are to be expected. These will be the more frequent if we are too insistent or too remote.

A fourteen-year-old pupil once said to me in a burst of confidence, "I am so unhappy. I don't seem to belong anywhere. Children my own age bore me and adults don't want me around." This pupil was living in two worlds. He was betwixt and between, one foot here, the other there. A most uncomfortable position.

A vexing problem for most piano teachers concerns the

large number of students who abandon the piano in their years of adolescence. It has been my experience that the less gifted are the first to lose interest. This is understandable. These students are usually in Junior High School, which places increased demands upon their few hours of leisure because of additional home work. If their aptitude for music is slight, the burden of practice becomes too great. Such students should be allowed to discontinue piano lessons if this is their wish, without recriminations from either parents or teacher.

It is often necessary to persuade parents that this is a wise attitude. In their eagerness for his musical education they may attempt a forcing process which I have found to be futile. Forcing can lead to a positive dislike and a cancelling of all future interest in music. Given freedom of choice, this student may at a later date express a desire to return to the piano. In some instances, even a year's absence will produce this happy result.

The repeated complaint registered by earnest parents lies in the words, "I want my child to have the music study which was denied me." Or, "My parents allowed me to drop the piano and I have always regretted it." We may sympathize but we must disagree, for unless these desires are shared by the child nothing will be accomplished. Time and money will be wasted. I have yet to see a successful result obtained by forcing piano study on an unwilling young person.

We must use a far different approach for the talented student who until adolescence has been our pride and joy. Will he be immune from the perils of this period? This has not been my experience. Talent is subject to the same pressures, often intensified by the additional ingredient of emotional sensitivity. I have in mind one of my most gifted students whose greatest joy was in his music. He practiced long hours with enthusiasm until the age of thirteen. School work presented no problem as he was highly intelligent. Then his interest began to wane. He became indolent, careless and moody. Practice hours were irregular or nonexistent. When he did go to the piano he spent the time aimlessly reading through one composition after another, learning nothing. The classics, formerly his delight, were rejected. His parents, who were very ambitious for him, became anxious and indignant, and he lived in a state of misery and rebellion.

Our friendship had been of long duration and he was able to give me his confidence to some degree. I permitted him to abandon all technical studies and substituted in place of the more demanding classics, music of a highly emotional content. Many students at this age are attracted to so-called popular music. I consider this a reasonable interest and never express disapproval. This boy, however, whose taste was normally fine, was not interested. He appeared to enjoy mildly the sentimental music chosen and began to spend more time at the piano. I did not demand from him a high standard of performance, and recitals were never suggested. He had previously taken great pleasure in playing publicly, but the adolescent often dreads being looked at or placed in a position of prominence. He is conscious of his sometimes unattractive appearance and may wish to go his solitary way.

This was the case with my student. It was a year of indulgence in which I was able to gain the cooperation of the bewildered parents through many conferences. Though the contact with my student was held by a very thin thread, it did not break. A number of lessons were spent in conversation rather than music. He grew more and more communicative and was able to relieve himself of some frustrations. I have found the time-worn adage, "this too will pass," to be of great value in consoling parents and as a self reminder. After a year or so of this irregular pattern, a slow and gradual change in attitude took place. There were indications that he was becoming more stable and tiring a bit of the too saccharine diet. The happy day arrived when he expressed a desire for more substantial fare. A few more months and his feet were on a new level of maturity. His return to playing in recitals was a natural sequence, but it was he who made the first request. I firmly believe that had I used any but the most silken discipline the period of trial would have extended far longer.

This experience taught me much but it must be borne in mind that each individual presents a different problem. There can be no fixed formula of procedure. Imagination must be constantly at work. Sympathy is not enough. Only by empathy can we hope to penetrate and understand this troubled young person. The barriers must be broken which stand between the mature adult and the child approaching adulthood.

In our great effort to make and maintain this desirable contact we cannot discard discipline completely. The young person is subject to the same laws of social conduct as the adult. Penalties follow transgressions. An appeal can be made to his growing maturity, for he dreads to be considered a child. While some compromise is necessary in the standard of perfection required for performance, certain basic rules must be observed. We cannot permit inaccuracy in reading.

I encourage such a student to listen to fine music whenever possible—recordings or concerts. These activities furnish a goal which, though perhaps unreached, will act as a stimulus to his own strivings. He will without effort absorb authentic interpretations which can have a subtle influence on his own too highly emotional performance. We should be indulgent of his eccentricities in this realm. His is an age of experiment, of fads, and only by trial and error will a proper balance be found. Robert Louis Stevenson has said, "Youth is wholly experimental." Music must allow a much needed outlet for the testing of perhaps bizarre ideas.

A heavy-handed teacher can stultify this healthy exploration. Great harm can be done by the suppression of adolescent instincts. Less desirable means of expression will inevitably be sought if they are driven underground. The powerful drives motivating the popular Rock and Roll groups whose influence is widespread, might have been diverted into saner channels.

A bright ray of hope is cast by a survey of teen-age delinquency which appeared in the *Saturday Review*. No delinquent was found who was a member of a school band, orchestra, or chorus. The need for stressing music curriculums in our schools is apparent. Any young person who can be made to accept the responsibilities of organized music activities finds comfort in group participation. His ego is served and attention taken away from his own particular awkward shyness. He is kept too busy to engage in gang wars and other forms of delinquency. He has his own gang

—a music gang. Many students form their own small ensemble groups stemming from the larger ones in which they have been active. Can we truthfully say that having his own "combo" and playing an occasional dance engagement will do him temporary or permanent harm? He may gain a small financial independence which could be sorely needed. I know from experience that the students in these groups work very hard. They have no time to roam the streets. I have seen them practice the piano even more industriously under the impetus of a job. They often become deeply interested in harmony since they must make arrangements for their little bands.

I am sometimes asked if a piano student should be allowed to play another instrument. I always give my consent, for the time lost in piano practice is less important than the value gained by the enlarging of musical activities during adolescence. The talented student will somehow find the time, while the less gifted one may actually do better with another instrument which may be less demanding. These are revolutionary ideas if compared with those of a former generation of dedicated but inflexible teachers, but I believe it is our duty to take a fresh and realistic view of the current situation. Our standards and goals remain fixed but as we gain in insight should we not allow a little time out for adolescence?

Granted that we have succeeded in keeping our student with us for piano lessons, we must now examine the compositions he will be interested in studying. I am constantly on the search for music which does not make too great a technical demand and which carries rhythmic and melodic charm plus appealing emotional content. I usually cut down technical studies to a minimum and at times have eliminated them altogether. This is not the period for Bach, Scarlatti, Mozart, etc., but there can be no generalization as to what every student will enjoy. I offer the simpler Waltzes, Preludes, Nocturnes and Polonaises of Chopin; Preludes of Rachmaninoff and Gershwin; short pieces by Tchaikovsky, Moszkowski, Albeniz, Granados, Tcherepnin; some Debussy and most certainly the Liebesträume and Consolations of Liszt. Compositions of contemporary composers can be found which answer the requirements. I frequently allow the student to choose his own materials, however farfetched the selections may be. I do not insist upon memorization unless this is his wish.

We cannot minimize our role as music teachers in this vexing period of adolescence. We have need of infinite patience in addition to all the other requisites previously outlined. But for our comfort we should remember that ours is not a new problem. It is to be noted that in almost every case of great talent or genius, the crucial point came around the age of fourteen. There are stories of a complete nervous collapse often due to a stern and exacting parent or teacher lacking in human understanding. In some situations the teen-age prodigy abandoned music completely for a period. He usually returned if his genius was sufficiently compelling, but who knows what harm was done meantime, and with what lasting effects? How many promising talents withered away, the true destiny of the possessor crushed and defeated by the harsh ignorance of his mentors?

Great musical gifts cannot of themselves guarantee success and happiness. The overwhelming responsibility of the teacher is to bring these gifts to fruition, praying for the wisdom to combine the proper proportion of understanding, affection, leniency, and discipline. Our first task is to hang on; the second, to be constantly on the alert for new approaches. We learn from our mistakes and here and there the rewards will come. They are often delayed and usually arrive when least expected. If one former student says, perhaps in later years, "It was you who helped me most in adolescence," we are repaid for our labor of love.

11. The Adult Student

> If we could have devised an arrangement for providing everybody with music in their home, perfect in quality, unlimited in quantity, suited to every mood, and beginning and ending at will, we should have considered the limit of human felicity already attained.
>
> Edward Bellamy

Thus spoke Edward Bellamy in 1887. Today the radio and television, unheard of in his time, would seem to answer his dream of "human felicity," not only in homes but in supermarkets, doctors' offices, beauty salons, sometimes to the point of saturation. Passive listening, however, does not always suffice. Many adults feel a deep-seated need for self-expression in some form of music for themselves as well as a "must" for their children.

No discussion of a piano teacher's experience can be complete if the needs and desires of a large group of adults who are not professional musicians are ignored. There are many mothers and fathers busily engaged in their respective activities who harbor a secret yearning to play the piano. Over and over, I am asked the questions, "Is it too late to begin? What are my chances for success?"

Arthur Loesser in his admirable book, *Men, Women, and Pianos*, throws a bright light on the place held by the amateur in the past. It is apparent as he traces the development of our present-day pianoforte which evolved from the clavecin and the harpsichord in the seventeenth century, that piano study was not confined to children. Many distinguished people prominent in various professions, as well as a busy housewife, Anna Magdalena Bach, embraced music heartily as performers.

Johann Sebastian Bach and his family gathered around the harpsichord in their evening sessions of music in which every member of the family, except the babes in arms, took part. I am sure they were encouraged to sing as soon as they could talk. Granted that this was the home of the greatest master of all time. But what of the mother, Anna Magdalena? She was expected to practice an instrument in addition to caring for their twenty-two children. She was apparently not very far advanced in music when Bach married her, for he compiled and composed the famous *Note-Book of Anna Magdalena Bach* for her benefit. Her activities present a striking example for the present-day mothers who consider themselves overworked and often find it difficult to practice with their own children.

The famous diarist Samuel Pepys was an ardent music lover and could play several instruments. He was constantly seeking and buying new instruments (and there were many varieties) which he found time to practice diligently. He was always on the lookout for new airs to be sung as well as played. It was a rare day in which some entry was not made pertaining to music. He even engaged his servants with an eye to their musical ability. Pepys with all his shortcomings presents a fine picture of a busy professional man (he held an important post in the Navy Office) who also found time to develop his avocation of music.

There are countless examples to be found if one searches

the pages of literary and musical history. Prince Esterhazy, Haydn's patron, was said to be an accomplished performer on the viola di bordone. Leopold I was a musician of considerable attainment. He was once told by his teacher that he should have been a professional performer. He answered, "Well, it doesn't matter. I'm better off as I am." If it is true that Nero fiddled while Rome burned, then he too must have found time to practice while attending to his ominous duties as emperor.

With these eminent personages in mind, should we not encourage a return to the piano for adults who may have had lessons in childhood but for various reasons let music fall by the wayside? The responsibilities of marriage or the professional careers in which they are engaged might have made them abandon any thought of further study. Should we receive a timid inquiry from such an adult, it is our cue to offer warm encouragement. The right words at such a moment may start this adult on an adventure which will open new vistas of musical enjoyment. He will experience a closer understanding of his child's development in the intricacies and difficulties of piano study. He will soon be able to play simple duets with his child and thus form a new bond. Most important, the parent is no longer an outsider, but a performer, even though on a limited scale. I have known children who were secretly teaching a parent at home, if it were merely letter names and the keys of the piano. Such a child is usually delighted when the parent has the courage to take unto himself the role of student.

We have failed in our profession of teaching if our lofty ideals are centered only on the talented child. I believe that the mysterious realm of music, boundless in its scope, should be available to all persons of any age expressing a desire to perform. We confess our own limitations if we exclude the adult who is of necessity a beginner. Ways and means should be sought to gear our teaching to his individual needs and limitations.

Granted there is a small amount of native ability, even though it has lain dormant for many years, any adult can enter into the project of making music if he so desires. He can experience the joys of participating rather than passive listening. He may face frustration and discouragement at first, but ask a mountain climber why he is willing to suffer the arduous discomforts of toiling up a seemingly unscalable cliff. He may not be able to tell you, but something makes him persist, and if defeated try all over again. It must be that he finds joy in the doing with the perhaps unattainable goal ever before him.

We sometimes assume that the adult beginner can obtain or even desire only a superficial knowledge of the piano, and we offer it to him as a mere hobby. This is a false premise and fraught with the germ of defeat. It is my firm conviction that there are unawakened potentialities resident in all men and women. Schools and colleges have until recently almost completely ignored the needs of adults for further education. It may be an unspoken but still a strong belief that when middle age is reached, learning time is over. Nothing could be further from the truth. The assets of maturity are many. They should be recognized and hitherto unused abilities set in motion. The process of learning need not stop with youth. Rather, it is a faculty which has been shown to persist into advanced old age. Chief Justice Holmes, who took up the study of Greek in his late eighties, was asked, "Why?" "Why to educate my mind, of course," was his answer.

However, as we approach the study of music, a far more potent reason than that of education presents itself. The professional man or woman, the busy parent, even though thoroughly engrossed, reaches out for something more. Education is not the complete answer, the adding of this course or that to keep the mind busy and reduce its boredom. The strong inner need of every individual is for expression of some kind, even though it may lie unrecognized or be given another name. Music and the allied arts offer the inimitable ingredient of emotional self-expression coupled with the growth of imaginative powers, once basic techniques have been established.

An intelligent adult not totally devoid of talent can learn to play the piano competently and with satisfaction through continuous and carefully directed study. It may be that he will never perform works which demand great technical skill, but there remains for him a wide field of piano literature which offers sustained interest and enjoyment in exploration. Moreover, he will listen to the performance of the masters with new pleasure and appreciation.

It must be granted that the advantages of adulthood are counterbalanced by motor disabilities. The finger muscles are apt to be less flexible, and the problem of obtaining wrist and arm relaxation is much more difficult. A child's hand, though weak and unmuscular, is still more malleable than that of the adult with more strongly developed but relatively unplastic muscles.

The late Leopold Godowsky, with whom I studied in my youth, taught us that brain was more important than muscle—that a piano was not played with the hands but with the mind which directed them. This idea should be instilled in adults who despair of ever obtaining sufficient technique. While it is true that technique *per se* cannot be ignored, still it is governed by the mental powers, and the mature adult has a tremendous advantage over the young child. Greater emphasis can be placed on technique as exercises will not so easily dull the adult's interest as that of the child. Many adults find actual pleasure in the simple act of moving their fingers, as they would in any other bodily exercise. When to this skill is added the ability to make of even a small folk tune a moment of musical expression, joy is increased a hundred fold.

I speak from experience for, in looking back over the years and listing the varieties of pupils I have taught, the names of many professional people come to mind. Besides mothers confined to the arduous task of child rearing and homemaking, my piano students have included two psychiatrists, the vice-president of a famous university, an official of the American Express Company, a postman, an electrical engineer, to name only a few. How did these busy people find time for daily practice? It is true that many of them could only practice one hour a day, but when this hour was adhered to consistently, there was recognized progress.

The adult, because of his presumptive background of musical appreciation, attentiveness, and mental development, can assimilate ideas more rapidly than the child. He will be able to absorb more at the lesson and practice with greater concentration. Thus progress will be faster. I do not believe in special materials for the adult beginner. As in learning any language, the same rules of grammar, pronunciation, and the building of vocabularies apply to students of all ages. I would naturally omit nursery rhymes and tunes which have a childish appeal, but there remains a great wealth of folk material which provides the best introduction to music for both child and adult. The simpler classics offer much esthetic pleasure for the adult, for with some musical background of listening he will appreciate and enjoy compositions that the young child might reject because of seeming austerity.

Thus far we have considered the adult who is practically a beginner at the piano. Another large group merits our attention: the men and women who attained some degree of proficiency in their youth, but who have since forsaken the piano. Surprises are in store for the enterprising teacher with the imagination to stimulate a renewed interest. This adult must be made to feel that much he believes lost can be regained. Scientists tell us that impressions once made never fade completely from the mind. Though the way back may be slow and at times painful, little by little former skills will return if the student is given careful and encouraging guidance. This experience may be compared to the re-studying of a foreign language learned in childhood. At first try, one draws a blank and is convinced that he must return to the very beginning. This is quickly proven untrue as forgotten words and phrases appear from the depths in which they have been hidden, unused.

The mature adult, though ill at ease at first, soon discovers that he approaches the piano with a new mental grasp and with renewed zest. He may wish to study a familiar favorite of his childhood and finds to his astonishment that it is now less difficult. The adult should be allowed free choice of selections. He will usually have the wisdom to drop something which is obviously beyond his present grasp, and the understanding teacher will substitute a composition less demanding.

A great obstacle to the adult's piano study lies in his unwillingness or inability to find the one small hour in his crowded day which can be laid aside for this new activity. Persuade him that it can be done—it is being done all the time by enthusiastic students. There is no schedule so burdened but what a space may be cleared if the desire is great enough. It is our pleasant task as teachers to increase and vivify this desire. When we consider the hours spent in idle chatter with well-meaning friends imposing on one's small amount of leisure, the often unprofitable moments of television viewing and newspaper perusal, it is evident that there is a replacement possible and for a more rewarding purpose. Time seems to be found for bowling, gardening, club meetings, etc. If the adult obtains great pleasure in his new pursuit of piano study, he will substitute the practice hour for these other recreations. I have known adults to become so absorbed that they even increased the prescribed hour from sheer delight in the doing.

A special word should be said for the busy mother. My current class includes ten mothers—one with five children, several with two or three little ones. These women have come to look upon their piano practice as the one refuge in the day. More important, they feel they are growing in an art which offers never ending possibilities. They have found something which is entirely their own. Their husbands are busily engaged in various professions, many winning recognition and acclaim. The mother often wakens to the knowledge that she is left behind, a household drudge. This makes for bitterness of spirit and can lead to great unhappiness and resentment. The husbands of my women students, almost without exception, exhibit surprise at first, followed by great pride as the wife slowly develops into a performing musician. She may well return to her former proficiency, but usually exceeds it. My little group meets several times each year with the husbands present for a formal evening of music. There is marked progress from year to year. I consider this a most pleasurable and valuable part of my professional life.

The crucial element in this undertaking is the way in which the all too short practice hour is spent. Specific directions must be given by the teacher. It is of great importance to devote five minutes of the time to sight reading. I advise my students to go through a collection of hymns, old songs, simple folk music, anything that may be at hand —to play one piece each day. Successful sight reading demands a going forward, without turning back to correct a mistake. After the key and time signatures are studied and a quick glance given to the page, the piece must be attempted without faltering. An astonishing facility will be acquired if this simple practice is adhered to every day for a long period of time.

The hour should be divided roughly into five sections. Sight reading, technical exercises, a page or two of new material, memorizing, and, finally, the performance. Memorizing is highly important, not only for the excellent mental training it requires, but for the ultimate musical performance for friends and family. The constant shifting of the eye from the page to the keyboard militates against an artistic result. The mind must so clearly know and retain the format of the composition, including every possible detail, that the final interpretation flows freely.

Extreme accuracy in learning must be stressed. Above all, slow practice. This is the most difficult rule of all to follow for pupils of any age. The mind cannot grasp the complexity of the countless details of a piano score if the pace is too rapid.

The ultimate word is concentration. Here the adult should excel, unless he lacks self-discipline. He cannot afford to lose one of his precious moments. His efforts must be so compressed into a clear pattern that the one hour will yield the ultimate in progress.

A family can be persuaded that this hour of the mother's practice is sacred. She must not be intruded upon. Easier said than done, but with firmness of purpose it can be accomplished. Habits, as we all know, are easily formed, but hard to break. The habit of practice can be made an integral part of each day.

If we, as teachers, are concerned only with the development of talent in the young, a large group of potential amateurs will be neglected. An amateur may be defined as a person who cultivates any study or art or other activity for personal pleasure instead of professionally or for gain. Our vision should be wide enough to include all earnest applicants who wish to share in our privileged realm of music.

12. The Child Prodigy

> Doing easily what others find difficult is talent, doing what is impossible for talent is genius.
>
> Henri-Frederic Amiel

A prodigy is a person endowed with extraordinary gifts or powers. He is a phenomenon, a wonder, a marvel, a miracle. But the word prodigy can also mean a curiosity, a freak of nature, even a monster. Research in the history of famous musicians reveals examples of these varied interpretations.

There is no satisfactory nor completely scientific explanation of the sudden emergence of a child prodigy. Music inheritance can often be traced to a parent or grandparent, though a generation may be skipped. Less frequently, genius will appear in a child who is the product of uneducated parents, with no known music in the background. Under all conditions, great talent is self-evident and usually demands expression at a very early age. A large responsibility rests with teachers and parents to guide and bring to fruition this strange and little understood gift.

Pitfalls are legion. True genius overrides conventional rules and blazes a new trail; it is a law unto itself. But however great the talent, tedious hours of practice are necessary for the development of technique. Is a small child capable of self-imposed discipline? Will his remarkable gifts be stifled and crushed by the imposition of adult dictatorship?

The study of famous child prodigies yields rich evidence of conflicting theories. There are appalling examples of the mistreatment of helpless victims. It can well be argued that the adult in control has sometimes been responsible for the "freak of nature"—the little monster. On the other hand, there are rare instances in which the young prodigy has been permitted to find his own path without hindrance, but with wise direction. Letters, biographies, and histories provide authentic sources of information which can be of great value to the teacher. This brief survey can offer only a few selected examples, but certain recurring patterns are traceable.

The Bach family presents a unique proof of musical inheritance. Music was the natural, successful and accepted profession for over two generations. Johann Sebastian Bach was exposed to music from infancy and evinced insatiable interest in it from the earliest age. It was his native habitat throughout his unspectacular life. He made his home at the age of ten with his brother Johann Christoph, where music was taken for granted. Although young Johann Sebastian was given some musical guidance by his brother, he was in the main self-taught. Authorities have sought in vain to explain Bach, but it appears impossible. He remains through the ages the supreme example of over-powering genius that still dominates the musical scene, past and present.

The Mozart family demonstrates a classic example of the relationship of father and son in the development of genius. Leopold the father was a musician in his own right, but in spite of his energy, ambition, and will, he was unable to realize his musical goal. He was destined to function as a Vice-Kapellmeister, and "There is no vacancy," became a familiar refrain in his professional life. His own failure was no doubt a contributing factor in his wholehearted ambition for his son.

Wolfgang Amadeus never attended school and had only one teacher in his entire life—his loving but oppressive father. He was completely under his direction for the first seventeen years of his life. He was already a virtuoso and composer at the age of six when he embarked on a three year concert tour. Mozart, though he appeared to be a happy, playful child, was obedient to his father's slightest wish. He was denied all initiative in his early years. It is highly probable that the father's complete domination explains in part Mozart's later inability to function sensibly and realistically in the world, once he had broken away from parental control. He was constantly on the move, changing residences time and again in his adult life. It is not difficult to connect his restlessness with the too early and constant concert tours when he was deprived of the security of one central home.

The years following his separation from his father at the age of seventeen were marked by continual poverty and illness. But though his genius flourished seemingly untouched by the constant trials to which he was subjected, it is a matter of conjecture whether his poor judgment in practical affairs may not have shortened his life.

Any theories we may have formed as to the early flowering of genius demonstrated in the lives of Bach and Mozart, are contradicted as we study the childhood of Beethoven. His was an atypical case. While his talent was obvious at an early age, he did not appear in public until he was eight, and waited three years before making his first short concert tour. His father sought to exploit him, no doubt influenced by Mozart's dazzling success as a child prodigy, but there is no evidence that Beethoven aroused any spectacular interest at this time. In contrast, Mozart was composing and playing at the age of four, and meeting with perpetual triumphs on his early concert tours.

Beethoven was hampered throughout his youth by his ignorant father, the insignificant and incompetent teachers who contributed little to his musical education, and the dismal pecuniary and moral conditions in his family that continued all his stormy life. However, the hardships of his youth taught him independence at an early age, and the lack of good instruction created a thirst for self-education. His genius overrode all obstacles, including serious illness and deafness.

The portrait of a child prodigy brightens as we contemplate Chopin's early years. One Christmas eve when he was six, he surprised everyone by going to the piano and playing tunes he had heard his mother play for guests. Moreover, he added his own embellishments. His mother and his beloved sister Ludwika became his first teachers; they were continually baffled by the demands of their exacting pupil.

Chopin was most fortunate in the musical environment provided by his parents. They were both superior amateur musicians; his mother a singer, his father a violinist and pianist. Chopin was not deprived of normal childhood pleasures. He was full of pranks and gaiety, and was never known to be bored. He did not seem to rebel against long hours of practice. Music was his joy, and the piano afforded him intense fascination. At the age of eight, he dictated marches and polonaises which his mother wrote down; one of the latter which he played at his first concert was published. It is to be noted that he did not ignore piano technique in these childhood years, and invented stretching exercises to increase the span of his hand.

Mendelssohn's childhood contains some contradictory elements. His relationship with his father whom he adored was one of extreme intimacy. Yet Felix had to submit unconditionally to the will of his parents. His teachers were selected, his practice supervised, as were his other studies. In spite of these disciplines it would seem that his musical growth was fairly normal and unimpeded.

An event of extreme importance took place when he was twenty; he was allowed to make an extensive tour of Europe alone. His letters reveal the tremendous development of his personality and his movement towards independent maturity. Mendelssohn until his death appeared to be a happy, brilliant, and beloved person.

A study of contemporary artists, successful in their chosen field, offers many similar examples—good and bad. Two in particular can be cited as offering contrasting childhoods—Jascha Heifetz and Ruth Slenczynska. Heifetz was blessed with parents who, though lacking in formal education themselves, had the wisdom to provide their children with a rich, cultural background. When Heifetz was three his father, a café violinist, brought him a quarter-size violin and began to teach him. His meteoric rise to fame needs no retelling. He became the pupil of Leopold Auer at the age of seven, and at eight made his first appearance with a symphony orchestra. Heifetz was very strictly brought up. He was required to practice four and sometimes six hours a day, and had to forego many of the natural pleasures of childhood. These rigors were inevitable and did not appear to harm him. They were counterbalanced by his warm and loving home life.

The tragic account of the early life of Ruth Slenczynska, the eminent pianist, offers a violent contrast. She was the victim of a brutal, ambitious father who decided arbitrarily before her birth that she was to be a musical prodigy. He attempted, as many other parents have done, to fulfill his own frustrated ambitions through his child. She gave her first concert at the age of four. From then on she was engaged in continuous tours both in this country and in Europe. She was deprived of all pleasure. Her insatiable father drove her with threats and savage beatings. She was kept a virtual prisoner, chained to the piano.

Eventually the gifted, sensitive girl broke down. Her health failed and it was only through the intervention of the Humane Society that she was liberated from her father at the age of fourteen. She abandoned music completely for a number of years and declared that she hated it. Fortunately, an early marriage and an understanding husband enabled her to rehabilitate herself as a musician and she resumed her professional life.

It is my good fortune to have in my current class of piano students, a child who exhibits unusual talent. She began piano study at the age of four and has seemed to follow in some degree the patterns described in the preceding histories. She was brought to me at the age of six and I felt very strongly that she had been forced far beyond her years both as to long hours of practice and far too difficult materials. This is a common error with many teachers dazzled by the startling qualities of great talent. They forget in their enthusiasm that they are still dealing with a tiny child. The first step with my little pupil was to obtain the confidence and support of the parents in the change of plan I wished to effect. I took her back to some of the simpler classics and stressed basic piano techniques. With the acquisition of greater skill she made rapid advancement and was able to leap hurdles impossible for a less gifted child. I have allowed her much latitude in the choice of compositions for which she has expressed a desire, providing they were not too demanding. Her taste is impeccable. I have encouraged the growth of her individual expression, attempting merely to guide her towards authentic interpretations. She has needed no encouragement to listen to all available good music for it is her joy.

It is characteristic of all prodigies that they delight in performance and this child is no exception. Her greatest happiness lies in playing. I give her many opportunities in informal recitals, avoiding any exploitation of her talent at this early age. She exhibits little nervousness before an audience—merely a natural excitement that does not detract from her performance. Stage fright seems to be unknown to her; she never plays better than when meeting the challenge of even a few listeners. Thus far, with her parents' wise cooperation, she has been able to carry on her school work with top marks, practice three hours daily, study music theory, and yet have some time for natural childhood recreations.

We may never encounter a true genius in the course of our teaching careers, but should one come our way, are we equipped to assume full responsibility for his development? We must not mistake talent for genius, nor must we be influenced by a parent convinced that his child is ready for the concert stage. A serious appraisal must be made. Talent in any given field shows itself in natural ability, in cleverness, and in aptitude. Genius, on the other hand, exhibits exceptional natural capacity for creative and original conceptions. Here we will find the master mind, the brilliant intellect and, in the field of the piano, a power of execution far beyond the capacity of a normally talented child. Genius has also been defined as the ability for taking pains. This I do not believe. The very young genius has not always taken pains in the early stages of development. He plays from some inner compulsion because he must—perhaps from the sheer joy of playing. He may be very careless as to details. It is the poor teacher who must take endless pains in guiding him in the rugged paths of discipline.

Once we have made a careful and, it is to be hoped, correct analysis of the incipient abilities of the alleged prodigy should one be brought to us, our pattern of procedure must be clearly outlined. Since this is no ordinary child, our handling of him must not be ordinary. He will be sure to tax our powers of invention, patience, and fortitude. He or his parents may abandon us mid-stream; for this we must be prepared. We cannot allow ourselves the luxury of emotional possessiveness. However, it is essential that teacher and child develop mutual respect and affection. This is possible if the parents do not interfere. We are powerless to develop our plan without their full consent, for it is they who will have the last word. Most parents are persuadable if convinced that the teacher is sincere and has the authority of experience. It is possible to give a gentle intimation that a too demanding, aggressive teacher or parent can cause the destruction of a budding genius.

The first practical factor is the allotment of time for practice. How many hours a day? If he is five or six, his schoolwork will present no difficulties. Great talent for music is usually accompanied by brilliant mental abilities. The prodigy will master quickly and easily the first grades at school, and will in all probability be bored. Piano practice can happily fill a need. As the child grows older, homework will increase. At this time a decision must be made. Should he be taken out of school in order to devote more time to music? If this is done, he must be tutored privately. This has been a familiar procedure in the past. I believe the results are questionable, and in some cases fatal. This child, if he possesses true genius is destined to be deprived of much that is natural and light-hearted. His childhood can never be carefree, but he should be allowed the companionship of other children he will find in school. His musical life for the most part will be spent with adults. A slower paced childhood development could result in a richer if somewhat delayed maturity.

Try as we will to proceed intelligently without undue pressure, the inexorable demands of such a child's talent will require a discipline beyond his years. We are on the horns of a dilemma; it is our stern duty to expand and fulfill the child's great gifts, and yet we yearn to give him all we can of youthful pleasures. We can only hope to find a happy balance. Recreation and outdoor exercise are often excluded in a rigid work schedule and parents should be urged to allow time for these activities, important to a child's health.

One question which looms large in the mind of every conscientious teacher concerns the development of technique. Too much emphasis on technique may stifle the expanding musical artistry; too much indulgence in emotional content may produce an interpretation lacking in keyboard control. Technical skill requires a slow, deep growth even for the prodigy. Tender muscles cannot be strained or forced; they must be coaxed with patience. The compositions chosen must be geared to the child's present attainment. We must be quick to note signs of fatigue if the material is too difficult, or boredom if it lacks challenge.

One inescapable fact emerges from any searching study of unusual talent. We cannot generalize, since every situation is unique. The best laid plans do not succeed with all pupils. We must be ever on the alert to abandon old, or create new, pathways as the need arises. Flexibility is the keynote, plus a constant awareness of the ever-changing young personalities we are guiding. Our reward lies in the extreme privilege of assisting in the growth of an artist.

13. How to Practice

> I believe that we are subject to the law of habit in consequence of the fact that we have bodies. The plasticity of the living matter of our nervous system, in short, is the reason why we do a thing with difficulty the first time, but soon do it more and more easily, and finally, with sufficient practice, do it semi-mechanically, or with hardly any consciousness at all. Our nervous systems have grown in the way in which they have been exercised, just as a sheet of paper or a coat once creased or folded, tends to fall forever afterward into the same identical folds. . . . The teacher's prime concern should be to ingrain into the pupil that assortment of habits that shall be most useful to him throughout life. . . . The great thing in all education is to make our nervous system our ally instead of our enemy. It is to fund and capitalize our acquisitions, and live at ease upon the interest of the fund. For this we must make automatic and habitual as early as possible, as many useful actions as we can, and carefully guard against the growing into ways that are likely to be disadvantageous.
>
> William James
> *Talks to Teachers*

The emotional content of music is an inevitable obstacle in the establishment of proper practice habits. Self-discipline is required from the student of whatever age. He must learn to abandon the desire to perform a composition in its entirety and instead study it piecemeal, usually a distasteful task. This is not to say that he is forbidden to read through the new work and try to grasp a general idea of its character. Then the real labor begins. Many repetitions of even one short phrase may be necessary in order to master the many details contained therein.

Many adults have never been able to accept the fact that practice and performance are widely separated activities. Each has a different goal. Practice should be thought of as a rehearsal in which the performer is able to stop and retrace his steps as often as he needs to. The final perfection of the uninterrupted performance depends upon the quality of the many practice hours; the self-criticism, care and patience employed in the long period of gestation. Emotional expression must be minimized while technical mastery is being developed. The mental processes of memory are also at work; only until these elements are mastered does the student attempt the all-absorbing study of interpretation.

How may good practice habits be established? If the student is a child, the first step should be a careful survey with pupil and parent of school hours, home duties, and outside activities. A mutual decision can then be reached as to how much time may reasonably be budgeted to practice. If we remain in ignorance of these vital facts, we may expect too much or too little. A frank discussion will also be very enlightening to a parent. The amount of practice time depends on the age of the child and what homework he is called upon to do each day. This will vary with the individual. The time selected should be when he is least tired. If family arrangements permit, early morning hours when the child is fresh are preferable. We cannot expect a small child to practice willingly immediately after school where he may have been confined all day. He should first be given a short period of play. Late evening practice is usually futile for the concentration of a sleepy and fatigued child will be at a low ebb. Nothing constructive can be accomplished under such unpromising conditions.

All practice should be alternated with periods of relaxation or change of activity. A young child should not be forced to sit at the piano longer than a half hour at one time. However, there are delightful exceptions. A gifted child may willingly increase this period through sheer interest and joy and can be given praise and encouragement in so doing.

Regular practice done every day at the same time is a most desirable habit. Compare this set hour with the daily deadlines he has to meet at school. He will have accepted the fact that he must not be tardy there. This discipline can also be exemplified by the necessity of catching a train at an exact moment. It is a far greater hardship for a child to be nagged constantly to practice, and to present evasions and arguments, than to adhere to an established and customary time. Some children can be interested in keeping a diary of daily practice and may take pride in this visual proof of their industry.

A common deterrent to good practice is lack of quiet and privacy. The piano is usually found in the living room, the center of family activities, and if there are other children about, the problem of concentration becomes acute. While we cannot be intrusive in our suggestions, it is salutary to point out the evils in these situations.

A few minutes should be spent at each lesson in sample practice with the teacher. A slow tempo is distasteful to most children whose natural pace is allegro, not andante. Children rarely walk—they run or skip. We must bear in mind that accuracy in reading and the many slow repetitions necessary in even short phrases are usually acquired habits, and must be established in the lesson. I have found this activity of value for adults as well as children. Only a mature and disciplined musician is able to extract the ultimate good from the hours at the piano. The highly gifted student is not exempt from these basic rules, even though he will grasp the musical content quickly.

A sparing use of the metronome is occasionally advised as the student progresses. It should be thought of as a governor, helpful in establishing a steady tempo. It can never of itself create a sense of rhythm. Excessive reliance on the metronome develops a mechanical beat which stultifies and devitalizes the elasticity needed for the artistic interpretation of a composition. The pupil who learns that it is only a crutch to be leaned on at times, will more readily overcome his instinctive distaste for the discipline of its temporary use. Specific directions should be given as to how and when it must be applied, and the exact tempo to be used.

Good practice habits form in time as the pupil is encouraged to listen and criticize himself; ears are soon dulled by mechanical repetitions, and every effort should be made to keep these fully alert.

Basic Practice Rules

1. Study the piece to be learned away from the piano before you try to play it. Note the tempo, time and key

signature, number and length of phrases, fingering, accidentals, staccato marks, etc. If rhythmical difficulties appear, clap out this particular measure.

2. Play through the composition in order to gain a superficial idea of it.
3. Omit any attempt at nuance for the first days.
4. Learn one phrase at a time.
5. Play slowly enough so that the eye can see and translate every detail to the brain and fingers. If the first visual impression is correct, each successive repetition of the phrase will hasten its technical mastery. Pretend you are making an impression in wax or clay. Once the groove is established it remains and tends to be followed.
6. Isolate the most difficult technical passages and repeat them a set number of times.
7. Do not consider interpretation until these preliminary steps have been mastered.

The success of the practice period and the forming of good habits lies with the parent, dependent upon an application of what the teacher has conveyed. If the parent can be persuaded to enter into the project with the child and to give guidance only when the need arises, pleasure instead of pain may be the reward for both.

What can be done in situations where the mother works away from home, or in families where there is no mother? Sometimes a father or housekeeper can be persuaded to take over this duty; but if no practice aid is available, and the child is very young, piano lessons are usually doomed to failure and should be delayed until the child is older. No child can be expected to practice alone the first year. I have never found an exception to this rule. However, I have sometimes successfully used an older student who, for a small fee, was willing to commence his own teaching experience through practice supervision.

14. Interpretation

> "I have noticed how often you use the words 'life' and 'living' when talking of interpretation."
>
> "This is because, on the one hand, I consider life as our great adviser and, on the other, for an artist, and especially for a performer, the essential problem is to produce a vital creation. We must reject all things that are not clear or may be artificial. By no means should one consider this rule an invitation to sloth; quite the contrary! Often we find that nothing is more difficult than to rediscover the marvellous simplicity of live shapes. First they must find an echo in our minds; after which we must pursue the work of investigation and elucidation of the different problems. An endless work. Years of study have confirmed the importance of this work. Every day I discover new things. . . .
> "Any performer who has not got a high conception of the work he has to play will probably use means which will not help his interpretation. It is all a question of equilibrium being maintained by good taste."
>
> Pablo Casals

The goal of musical performance is neither intellectual understanding nor technical virtuosity, but their artistic synthesis by means of the imagination. Interpretation, by which music comes alive, can be achieved only through these media. The intrinsically meaningless notes which confront the student can be translated into sound by a mere mechanical manipulation of the piano keys, an arithmetical application of time values, and some mastery of piano technique. But interpretation adds feeling and emotion, and brings these elements into an expressive pattern. The performer then is able to connect composer and audience with a highly personal and creative link. He must make sure that this link follows the composer's intent. Once it has been understood it must be followed scrupulously, though no two musicians will ever produce identical interpretations of the same composition.

What is good taste? Is it a natural gift? Are we born with it? If not, can it be acquired? It is helpful to attempt to analyze what good taste may be in fields other than music. Resourceful teachers will find examples illustrative of many musical ideas from their own, or the student's daily life. Good taste in clothes or in manners, furnish a simple starting point. A child first learns by imitation. If his environment is a fine one, he will unconsciously absorb much of what he sees or hears through family exposure. This process does not stop with childhood, but continues through adult life. Whatever the background, anyone alert to his surroundings can be aided if he has a growing perception of what is worthy of imitation and, more important, what is appropriate. A vital role of the teacher is to direct the pupil's attention toward these things.

A sad tendency among some musicians is to be interested chiefly in their own instrument, neglecting the valuable lessons to be learned from the related fields of music, plus the fine arts of painting, sculpture, dancing, drama, and literature. At the earliest possible age, the student, if he is to become a well-rounded musician, should be taught that his instrument, the piano, is only a part of a whole. Here the teacher's influence is very great. If he lacks interest and enthusiasm for these vital adjuncts, he cannot expect his student to acquire them quickly and unaided.

Style is an integral part of interpretation. Its many definitions make it a perennially controversial topic among artists. It may be broadly defined as a characteristic mode or form of construction or execution in any art or work; a distinctive artistry is also implied. Every piece of music has its own particular style which must be related to the historical background of the period in which it was composed. Traditional interpretations which present an authentic style can be studied in recordings of the masters. An examination of musical literature by established authorities is of great value. One may find a sentence or paragraph which will cast a bright light on a vexing problem. It is not always easy to determine from the printed score the composer's true intent. The works of Bach and Chopin, to cite two examples, require completely different approaches. The inexperienced student cannot be expected to understand these extremes in style without guidance by his teacher and all other available sources.

Interpretation is sometimes ignored in the very early stages of study for a young child. This is a mistake. In spite of the bewildering difficulties of note learning, rhythmic values and the technical coordination demanded by the piano, it is not only possible but essential that some hint be given as to the musical nature or style of the first folk tunes studied. The child will understand them, perhaps better than you, the adult, since they are primarily songs with titles and words which appeal to his imagination; they are near his world through his familiarity with nursery rhymes.

There are marching songs which demand a vigorous,

robust treatment, such as "The British Grenadiers," "The Campbells Are Coming." A reference to the country and the occasion for which they were written brings them into focus. Innumerable cradle songs from all countries provide a direct contrast in treatment and offer an opportunity for small nuances. Descriptive songs which feature bells, clocks, the rain, etc., by means of repetitive patterns, are always popular. Alternate these various types, one with the other, in order that the child will gradually develop a feeling for each new style as it is presented, together with some knowledge of the technical means essential to their interpretation.

Duets offer an additional means of musical growth at this time. The pupil's part is usually very simple, but by playing with his teacher he is guided without words to produce the proper mood. He will be given strong rhythmic support and may instinctively copy the nuances he hears in the teacher's playing. Imitation is not an evil in this situation for he may be unable to produce a musical result without support. The gifted child may find his greatest joy in this weekly ensemble activity.

A new style is introduced with the early classics through small menuets and gavottes of Bach and Mozart. These compositions are used as examples of musical forms in which neither words nor descriptive titles are necessary as a guide to interpretation. The child will probably know something of the colonial period through school programs. Talk about the costumes worn, the powdered wigs, the hooped skirts. Then play a menuet letting the child experience the slow, stately rhythm. Suggest that the lady must be allowed time to curtsy, the gentleman to bow.

The true classic style follows with the early Sonatinas, Rondos, and Variations in which both form and content are analyzed. This early study is a direct pathway to more advanced compositions. A legitimate way of arousing the perceptions in the more abstract forms could come through the teacher's playing—but a word of caution. Beware of playing too much for a young child. He may imitate your performance in parrot fashion, and his own imagination remain inert.

The simpler compositions of Gretchaninoff, Tchaikovsky, Schumann, Grieg, offer still further opportunity for the expansion of the child's creative expression. The works of these so-called romantic composers call for subjective treatment. They require a sensitivity to poetic titles and provide an opportunity for the child's own imagination to function. This can be a fascinating period of advancement, for we may now see evidence of his individual talent.

The foundation of sound musical taste and interpretation lies in the art of listening to fine music wherever it can be heard. The pianist can learn from the best in chamber music and orchestral performances; from an accomplished singer, cellist or violinist. There are abundant opportunities at hand. Commensurate with the student's power of absorption, will he acquire depth and authenticity of performance.

15. Recitals

> You say you are afraid of public performance. An audience is only the multiplication of one person. Play to him.
>
> Frédéric Chopin

No guaranteed remedy exists which will ensure a performer against that arch enemy—stage fright. There are many renowned and mature artists who will testify to this fact. Experience alone reduces the physical distress—moist and trembling hands and too fast a heart beat. The coordination of mind, emotions and physical control must carry the day if a beautiful interpretation is to be presented. Great value lies in an early audience exposure for young children.

Most children take great pride in being able to play their first small pieces for friends at home or at school. There is no greater incentive to the perfection of a composition than to implant the idea that it will find an appreciative if small audience. Instead of one formal, yearly recital—unfortunately still in vogue with some teachers—times should be set aside for informal gatherings which in the beginning can be termed class lessons. If the teacher's class is large and contains children of varying ages, it is wise to separate them into groups of a relative level of advancement. However, this technique need not be adhered to rigidly. Younger children will be stimulated by hearing occasional performances by more advanced students.

Duets with the teacher are the best vehicles for a child's first public performance, either in class lessons or recitals. The teacher can thus unobtrusively, but effectively, guard against a failure which may leave an ineradicable scar. Much of his future happiness in, and his desire for performance, depend upon the pleasant memories of his first experience. It is not unusual for a child who thinks he has failed to state that he will never play again in a recital. Lapses in memory are avoided by having the notes of the duet before him. Rhythm is stabilized and interpretation guided by the teacher's proximity, and nervous excitement is thus greatly reduced.

The timid child who shies away at the mention of playing in public should not be forced to it. Give up the idea at once if he seems really afraid, and encourage the child to come to a recital as a listener. The desire to take part is often kindled by observing his friends in action as he comes to realize that he is missing a pleasurable activity. No child enjoys the feeling that he is being left out. If no pressure is put upon him, he will very probably ask that he, too, may play the next time. The initiative which effectively overcomes his fear must be his own. An over-ambitious mother or a too demanding teacher can be strong deterrents.

There is a small percentage of children who, no matter how carefully the approach is made, reject public performance. These children may have little musical aptitude, or they are temperamentally timid and insecure. On either basis, no child can be expected to enjoy playing for an audience if he lacks self-confidence. Never force recitals upon the reluctant child. Instead, seek the cause of, and the remedy for, his fears.

After several recitals in which the child has played duets only, he should be ready for a group of solo folk tunes. Even these are best prefaced by one duet, which will carry on a familiar pattern and establish the confidence he has been taught to experience with the teacher by his side. He can then more easily assume full responsibility for his initial attempt at solos. These should be relatively simple; choose pieces which do not tax all his resources.

Over-preparation, namely, learning a piece too far in advance of the recital date, is an evil to be avoided. A child's retentive powers are short and he will inevitably fall into a rote pattern if kept too long on a composition. This is asking for memory failure which, when it occurs in public, is a disaster for a child.

Much depends upon our attitude after a poor performance, which is sure to happen occasionally in spite of all our care. His own distress will be great. I never discuss his mistakes until the following lesson. It is not difficult to find an encouraging word without being insincere, and to point out that not all games are won. He must be prepared to be a good loser, and resolve to correct obvious errors in preparation. On our part we must not lose sight of the fact that it is impossible to eradicate completely the nervous excitability which plagues most performers at whatever stage of advancement.

I have found it helpful to dramatize in the studio what will actually take place in the recital. Say to the child, "Let's pretend that today is the recital. Now, the program tells you that you are next. Rise and walk rather slowly to the piano. Do not run. Be sure you are comfortably seated, with the bench at the right distance from the piano. Do not begin to play until your fingers are over the right keys. Wait until you have thought through the rhythm of the first measure. Do not take your eyes from your hands while playing even though there may be disturbances or unexpected noises in the room. Do not run from the piano when you have finished. Rise and make a bow to the audience when they applaud. Clapping their hands is their way of telling you that they have enjoyed your playing. Your bow is a way of saying 'thank you.' "

If a group of pieces is played, teach the child to take his hands from the piano after each one, and wait a few seconds before beginning the next. Because of excitement, the natural tendency is to run one piece into the other. This rehearsal should be gone through several times, and repeated at home with perhaps the father as the audience. No matter how careful the preparation, the first recital is a strain upon the child's sensibilities.

Self-confidence and poise will gradually develop through successive performances. The praise and encouragement received from parent, teacher, and friends provide the greatest incentive for future efforts. It is a rare child who does not ask when he may play again. A second benefit derived from attendance at informal recitals lies in the child's development as listener as well as performer. These occasions often provide the only opportunity he has for hearing piano music at his own level. The playing will be of varying degrees of excellence and children can be taught at an early age to distinguish the good from the bad. Their own playing will be benefited as perceptiveness increases.

Encourage pupils to offer praise to their fellow students for good performances. There is no better way to establish friendship, to show interest in, and appreciation for the efforts of others. These qualities are sometimes sadly lacking in adult musicians whose attention was never directed outwards to the achievements of contemporaries.

Students should be urged to play at school whenever asked and be provided at all times with a suitable composition. Light, attractive pieces of not too serious a nature are the best selections, though the early classics are often welcomed by enterprising school teachers who plan music appreciation programs. A pupil, not the parent or teacher, should make his own choice of recital material. He will invariably choose his favorite. Never force him to play a composition in public that is not dear to his heart. In this area we can afford to be highly permissive. This is a required ingredient for his success.

The gifted student whose talents lie in the direction of the concert field will have had ample preparation in the plan outlined here. He should be ready for an unpretentious solo recital, perhaps in his last years of high school. He is then ready to take his place in the world of music as a performing musician.

16. Reconstruction Problems

> For as steel is imprinted in the soft wax, so learning is engraven in ye minde of an young Impe.
>
> John Lyly

The teacher who has established a definite plan for the early years of music study will find it an easy and delightful task to teach promising beginners. He will, however, acquire students of all ages who have some previous knowledge of the piano. The instruction of many of these may have been faulty and unadaptable to the plan in effect. Bad habits and misconceptions as to proper technical and musical approach may have been firmly entrenched, the materials used cheap in quality and far too difficult for their attainment.

In such cases, instead of the relatively simple job of building a firm musical foundation from nothing, the faulty structure must be torn down and the painful task of rebuilding begun—the sort of underclearance which an architect must effect before his new edifice can be erected, however inspired and justified his plans.

Unhappily, this situation is all too common. Both parent and child should be spared the full realization that much that has been learned is of little value and that some, if not all of it, is dross. This sad truth must be revealed slowly. Profound discouragement and a decision to abandon the piano may result if the new teacher at once displays too high-handed and critical an attitude. One encouraging factor lies in the reason for the new teacher having been chosen. This can be dissatisfaction with the old. It is helpful in the first lesson to compare a change of teachers with a change of doctors when different medicines and treatments are prescribed, often for the same condition.

Suggest to the parent that certain variations in approach may improve the child's playing. Make the necessary constructive criticism gently and gradually, but nonetheless effectively. Avoid any disparagement of the former teacher. Be sure to recognize and comment on any good that has been attained. Praise that which can still be retained. Conceal your dismay at the inferior compositions the pupil may have been given. Do not make too radical a change in materials. Instead, try to find for the first assignment works which are similar but slightly better in quality. I have often abandoned temporarily the usual classic materials and substituted instead a variety of light, attractive pieces of some musical merit calculated to attract the child's interest. Taste and appreciation for the classics cannot be forced, but must be allowed to develop slowly. New ideas of technique and interpretation can be acquired far more quickly if the medium used is not too foreign to the child's previous experience.

Even though the proper materials have been found, the teacher's most difficult task is yet to be done. A careful analysis of the pupil's playing may reveal essential lacks. These must be approached in order of their importance. If he reads slowly and inaccurately, special exercises in note review and sight reading must be established. Poor rhythmic concepts demand an immediate correction. Do not dwell upon the obvious faults to the exclusion of the musical content, or you may lose your pupil by reason of his sheer rebellion. Explain that these basic ideas must be established since they have hitherto been omitted from his instruction. The pupil who has been taught merely to perform, but who has not been given the means, must be allowed time for his mind and his ears to catch up with his fingers.

Now and then one finds a superior parent and child who seem at the outset able and perhaps eager to accept the discouraging truth that they must start over again from the beginning. These are the pupils who have been aware that something was amiss in their former studies and yearn for improvement. When this proves to be the case, much time will be gained by a ruthless abandonment of what has been erroneously taught and a fresh start made from scratch. But such admirable students and parents are rare. These ameliorations of the teacher's task will occur infrequently. We must not mistake a willingness to go along for a full and understanding compliance.

Another difficult area of reconstruction comes when we are faced with bad piano technique. This presents a wide-open field in which every conceivable weedy fault may flourish. Not only must the unfortunate pupil be taught what to do and how to cultivate the soil, but he must unlearn and eradicate much of what he has with much labor acquired.

Simplify this process by starting with not more than one or two basic ideas. The principle of relaxation is often lacking. In my experience it is the one thing most commonly neglected and the one on which the most emphasis should be placed. It is often the greatest contributory cause of bad technique. Appropriate exercises, both away from and at the piano, that will help to establish a relaxed arm and shoulder, should be invented.

The pupil with a faulty hand position must be re-educated through plastic molding of the hand at each lesson. Discuss the problem freely; encourage him to take a long-range view of the issue. Note and give instant credit for any slight improvement. Countless patient repetitions are necessary to make the pupil aware of his deficiencies and of his ability to recognize and overcome them.

A salutary factor in the establishment of new techniques is the pupil's own observation of other students who have mastered these principles in some degree. This idea is also directly applicable to the enlargement of repertoire and the development of finer musical taste. Create opportunities for the new student to hear and observe his fellow classmates who are farther along the road. New disciplines will be eased and made more acceptable if he sees others obviously benefiting. Pupils of any age sometimes learn more easily from each other than from the teacher. I have used an older pupil many times for the purpose of setting the new one on the right track.

The process of reconstruction presents one of the most vexing yet challenging aspects of all teaching. We must not be dismayed if we lose some pupils along the way. The errors may be too deeply entrenched, the student unwilling to accept the seemingly cruel but necessary new disciplines. In addition, his talent and interest may not be keen enough to carry him through this difficult period. If our most earnest efforts fail, we should advise that he abandon the project or seek elsewhere for a less demanding teacher. Frankness with both parent and child is an honorable necessity.

However, there is great satisfaction for every one concerned if we are successful in steering a gifted student into the proper paths, no matter how long the period of reconstruction may take. Here, as in every teaching situation, confidence, respect, and, it is to be hoped, some affection for the new teacher are vital requisites.

17. Building a Class

> Cast thy bread upon the waters: for thou shalt find it after many days.
>
> Ecclesiastes 11:1

How does a young teacher attract pupils to himself? Where are they to be found? How can he persuade parents that besides the years of fine training in performance, he is equipped to teach their children, since he lacks experience which some consider essential. The doctor who awaits his first patient has a similar anxiety. Professional ethics prohibit any blatant advertisement of their qualifications. By what legitimate means can our abilities be made known to the community in which we hope to make our livelihood?

An affiliation with a school, public or private, should be sought if no school of music exists. A group or club interested in the fine arts may be willing to assist. The name of a recognized institution is a valuable recommendation for the unknown professional person.

A public announcement can be made through newspapers or private mailing lists. It should state that the teacher is opening a piano studio—the address and phone number—a brief statement of degrees held or specific training. In order to obtain pupils quickly, he may indicate a willingness to go to the home to give the lesson, but this is ill advised unless there is no other solution. It is important that lessons eventually be given in a studio where quiet and privacy can be assured, and where time in transportation for the teacher can be saved. But parents are also interested in saving their own time. It is the teacher who should make the sacrifice until his career is well launched, since pupils are a prime necessity.

The ability to make social contacts is a vital factor in building a class. You will be judged by your personal appearance and the qualities of friendliness and interest which you as a newcomer display before you are even given a chance to perform. Lacking these assets you may well be condemned, unheard, and untried. Do not hold yourself aloof; enter into the activities of the community. Remember that you are on trial and that your worth as a person must be demonstrated in some small measure before you will be allowed to prove your professional abilities.

Contribute your services as a pianist whenever possible. The readiness to perform is a fruitful means of self-advertisement. While ability and willingness are not the only ways to attract pupils, they can be the opening wedge in making new acquaintances and friends. From this group may come your first pupils. Welcome whoever enrolls as your student, however unpromising he may appear. Through him you may find others. The enthusiasm of even one pupil will provide a potent publicity, for enthusiasm is essentially contagious. This first pupil and his parents will be very apt to recommend you to others. Your ultimate success as a teacher is reasonably secure if their interest and happiness in piano study can be sustained.

"By their fruits ye shall know them" can truly be said of the teaching profession. Your unquestionable ability to teach will be proven only with the passage of time. If you can produce one pupil who plays beautifully, that pupil's performance will speak more loudly than any words of praise of yours or your friends.

I am often asked advice as to the young teacher's fee. It should depend in part upon what is asked by established teachers in the community. If the scale is very low, it may be advisable to increase it slightly by virtue of the superior training you may have had. But do not forget that you may be under suspicion because of your youth and lack of teaching experience. Parents must be convinced that you have a superior equipment before they will consent to a greater expenditure of money. It is far better to have a flourishing class for the first year of teaching, thereby gaining valuable experience, than to set too high a price on your services and lack pupils. The fee for lessons can be raised gradually with successive years as your reputation grows.

It is assumed that your methods are representative of the best modern piano pedagogy, but something more is needed if you are to attract pupils. If your class is small in the beginning, you will accordingly have one valuable commodity denied an older teacher with a more crowded schedule. That precious and rare commodity is time.

What can you give your pupils besides the meager thirty-minute lesson for which they pay?

Any teacher wholeheartedly interested in his profession must realize that his duties are not ended with one weekly lesson. He must sell that much of his time in order to make a living wage. But it is the overflow of his interest, demonstrated in countless ways, which makes of his business in life, not a trade, but a creative art, capable of infinite expansion. The intangibles of teaching are above price, and cannot be purchased or paid for. The teacher who demands a fee for every minute spent with his students will go through life poverty-stricken in spirit.

It is not necessary to teach long hours of overtime to prove an interest—in fact, the too conscientious teacher often does harm by practicing laboriously with his pupil instead of teaching him to stand on his own feet. Interest can be much more profitably expressed if opportunities are offered for private conferences with parents and pupils as the need arises—by group discussions, class lessons, duet and ensemble playing with other instruments which are available, a weekly hour of theory given gratis, and small recitals. Many of these activities can be accomplished with an actual condensation of time, since they concern a group and need not be repeated to each individual. A note of warning—do not expect gratitude for these extra services. Unfortunately, they are often accepted without a word of thanks. If you feel that you are being imposed upon in this respect, you may perhaps be doing too much for the individual. A gentle pointing up of what the pupil is actually receiving may be in order. Your reward will come indirectly through the development of the talent with which you may be dealing. This, in the end, will speak loudly for your ability as a teacher.

Many communities abound in piano teachers. The self-righteous young teacher may be appalled at the results of their teaching. Never give voice to this impression. These same teachers may have satisfied their students who knew no better approach. Too aggressive an attitude on the part of the newcomer armed with what he believes to be the only method will create suspicion and active hostility. His progressive ideas may well be a militant reproach to the resident teacher dependent upon pupils for his own livelihood. Every effort should be made to establish as friendly a relationship as possible. There is no better way to create ill-feeling than to flaunt what you believe to be a unique system with an attitude of superiority.

The building of a permanent class cannot be accomplished in one or two years. Even a salaried position in a school of music does not insure its continuance. Every teacher has to prove his ability to hold his class and gain other students, whether his pupils must be sought for or handed to him. This can be accomplished only with complete integrity, and willingness to place the student's interests above his own personal ambition for performance. As was indicated in an earlier chapter, the mature musician can do both things, but in the outset of his career he would do well to place the emphasis on giving, not taking.

18. Why Pupils Fail

> If a man has talent and cannot use it, he has failed. If he has a talent and uses only half of it, he has partly failed. If he has a talent and learns somehow to use the whole of it, he has gloriously succeeded, and won a satisfaction and triumph few men have ever known.
>
> Thomas Wolfe

Piano study is abandoned by a large number of students. They and their parents are left with a sense of failure, sometimes with just cause. I believe it to be the duty of every thoughtful teacher to ask, "Why?" The next step is to try to discover the answer. A variety of reasons emerge —as many as there are varying types of students.

Lack of musical aptitude is a common cause. Music has an attraction for many people of all ages. They are not always content to listen; they would like to perform as well. After an enthusiastic beginning, they may discover to their sorrow that they lack essential aptitudes. Discouragement is sure to follow. If the situation seems hopeless, a sincere teacher will, through frank discussion, attempt to steer this student into other fields of self-expression. This is a relatively simple solution compared with the complexities presented by those who have some innate ability but who fail nevertheless.

We, as well as the student, are often victims of bad teaching done by former teachers. There are feeble practitioners in every profession including our own. It is a true if sad admission that some teachers turn pupils away from the piano by their antiquated methods, the poor materials used, and most of all by their lack of inspiration and a distaste for their job. I have known adults whose natural impulses towards music were killed in youth by a severe and unloving teacher. The mark of failure and inferiority still remained, a bitter memory which prevented their making any further attempt. The imprint of any teacher, by virtue of the authority placed in him, is deep and permanent. Could it also be true that we ourselves are sometimes responsible for the student's failure? This painful question should be asked when we are not successful in sustaining interest.

It is considered ethically wrong to denounce another colleague. If we are convinced that the student must be given a basically new approach, perhaps in opposition to what he has been taught, we must proceed with tact and sensitivity. The difficult process of reconstruction must be kept as impersonal as possible. If he retains a deep-seated loyalty to his former teacher, resentment may follow and we cannot succeed.

Age is an important issue in success or failure. Unless a child exhibits great interest in the piano and demands lessons, they should not be attempted too early. I have seen children at the age of four or five turn from the piano with distaste when, after the first initial excitement, the inevitable difficulties arose. The parent may complain of the lack of interest shown, but the experienced teacher will know that too much had been expected too soon. As was indicated in an earlier chapter, one or two years spent in the fundamentals of music before instrumental study, would give him the proper background and let him ripen in age. Even with the highly talented child for whom concessions must be made, we still must proceed with caution. We cannot evade early disciplines which must be commensurate with the child's tender years.

Too late a beginning is also a great handicap. A child who starts lessons when he is twelve is often very conscious that younger children have far surpassed him and he despairs of ever catching up. Unless his interest and determination are keen, he is apt to abandon the project.

The family situation has a sharp bearing on the ultimate result. Too stern demands from an overbearing or aggressive parent, or the opposite—complete permissiveness—can thwart our best-laid plans. The television can be named the arch enemy in homes where its unlimited use is permitted, especially during practice hours when the inevitable result is loss of concentration, which leads directly to loss of interest. Other children can also furnish unwanted distractions. It must always be remembered that practice time is taken from a child's playtime. If he is a boy with a keen interest in sports, rebellion may follow as a natural sequence unless we are able to make the piano a counter-attraction. We may indeed despair of finding solutions to these baffling problems unless parent and teacher are working together in harmony. Alone, we would need superhuman powers.

The child's state of health and his individual temperament must also be considered. A delicate, physically weak child may find the extra burden of piano practice too irksome. Another may, because of timidity and shyness, reject the attempt which forces him into self-expression.

This attitude can also be caused by an older sister or brother who evinces greater abilities which make the less gifted one feel inferior. It is always a difficult task to teach piano to several children in the same family and keep them all happy, as their aptitudes will vary. I have often suggested another instrument for the weaker one in such cases. This may give him a healthy feeling of superiority as he strikes out in a new path which is his alone. A change of instrument is also advisable for a child who lacks the physical coordination necessary for piano technique. A flute, clarinet, or horn presents fewer difficulties, and will enable him to take part later in small orchestras and bands.

Drop-outs are frequent in the period of adolescence. Causes and remedies were explored in Chapter 10.

Perhaps our greatest responsibility lies with the moderately gifted but overly ambitious student, determined on a concert career. Talent alone is no guarantee of success. Music centers to which students gravitate can be graveyards of musical aspirations. They are filled with embittered musicians who are signal failures in their chosen profession. "Ambition without justifying cause" might well be their epitaph. More scholarship grants for student study are available now than ever before in our history, but competition is keener. Rewards will go to those with outstanding abilities. What of the many who have been misguided by an over-enthusiastic teacher into a false exaggeration of their talent?

The student, after great sacrifices, arrives with high ambition only to be faced with the crushing realization that years have been spent in a lost cause. He is refused admission to the school of his choice and perhaps given a frank analysis of his deficiencies. He is left adrift to face despair unless he has a powerful determination to overcome all seeming obstacles. The bitter experience of failure could have been avoided if a discerning teacher in the early years of high school had given him wiser counsel. I think a long time before advising any student to enter the profession of music. I must be thoroughly convinced of his talent, intelligence, and character.

There are other less demanding areas in which a musician may function happily without virtuosity. It is our responsibility to explore these possibilities for a student intent upon some form of musical life. The choice of a career can be determined only by a correct evaluation of his potentialities. I have found it helpful for a student of moderate gifts to suggest Public School Education, Music History, Theory in its many branches, or music as a major subject in a Fine Arts college. The field of music offers a variety of opportunities for a student who has some ability and an unquenchable desire to spend his life in music. It is true that our advice is not always taken by a young person who persists in his lofty aims, all evidence to the contrary. We must retreat gracefully if our words are of no avail. This student has to prove himself and may surprise us by the development of latent, hidden resources. We cannot claim omnipotence.

A primary function of the true teacher is to encourage and discourage, to know when and how. There is no known alchemy to prevent failures nor create success. Our joyful reward comes when we are able to divert a seeming failure into some degree of achievement and bring to fruition a fine talent.

19. Piano Literature

> Listen most attentively to all popular songs: they are a mine of most charming melodies, and afford an insight into the character of different nations. You must not circulate bad compositions: on the contrary, you must suppress them. Regard it as something abominable to meddle with the pieces of good writers either by alteration, omissions, or by the introduction of new-fangled ornaments. This is the greatest indignity you can inflict on art.
>
> Robert Schumann
> *Maxims for Young Musicians*

A larger quantity of music, good and bad, has been written for the piano than for any other instrument. This field of literature ranges so extensively that the young teacher may well be bewildered in choosing what is best for each pupil. Particular care must be used in the selection of materials for the first years of study. Just as the technical demands must be commensurate with the pupil's means, so the emotional content of the composition should be within his understanding. This principle is used by all thoughtful parents and teachers in the books recommended for the child to read.

Elimination is the first step in clarification. Decide primarily what you will *not* teach. An examination of current catalogues of piano literature draws forth the following broad generalizations.

1. Do not teach the so-called "Method Books" in which a dogmatic system is followed blindly.
2. Do not teach music cheap in quality which aims merely to amuse the pupil. Every conceivable device will be found to attract his eye and engage his attention. Silly jingles and manufactured tunes often take the place of simple, authentic folk tunes. Many current books are an insult to the intelligence and innate musicality of children. It is a proven fallacy that students must be cajoled with inferior materials in order to enjoy music lessons. They will find as much if not more pleasure and stimulation in fine music if exposed to it from the start. Third-rate compositions can exert a pernicious influence on their still plastic musical taste.
3. Do not teach simplified or distorted arrangements of the classics. Whole series which have unfortunately attained great popularity are built on the mutilation of the original score. This is a musical crime, condemned by every musician of integrity.
4. Do not teach pieces of a programatic nature which lack any qualifications of a good composition. Their chief allure may lie in a catchy title bearing little relation to the unoriginal and meager musical content. Thousands of these compositions are ground out each year as if by a mill. The deluded teacher who seeks for novelties to stimulate his pupil's interest will receive a poor reward.
5. Do not teach music containing difficulties beyond the grade level for which it was supposedly written. This dictum is applicable to many classics written for children. Great composers have failed frequently to recognize the technical limitations of a child. Many "Albums for the Young" are unusable until the child is no longer young. A

student in the intermediate grades resents the words "Child," "Young," "Easy" on titles of works designed for his age, but not allowing for his pride and ambition. It is a rare child who does not wish you to think he is older than he is.

6. Do not teach technical studies which are lengthy and monotonous. If pure technique is offered in any but very small doses, strain and tension instead of fluency will be the net result.

7. Do not teach music which though fine in quality is too serious and mature in conception for a child's present grasp.

8. Do not teach music by contemporary composers of so extreme an idiom as to be distasteful to children as yet ungrounded in classic literature.

What remains after these many eliminations? Our first duty and one of paramount importance is to select by careful examination the best possible and authentic editions, our intent being to discover what the composer actually wrote. We cannot accept what a misguided editor saw fit to change according to his own inadequate ideas.

The following suggestions are gleaned from many years of trial and error in the author's experience. *Do teach:*

1. Superior collections of folk songs. Select those which appeal to the child's imagination and which have skillful harmonic arrangements. They should contain interesting melodic and rhythmic content. The individual method of each teacher can be applied to these materials and adjusted in a variety of ways to the needs of the student. Duets should be used freely through the first years of study. They enhance interest and offer a first experience in ensemble playing.

2. The simpler compositions of classic composers in their original forms. There is an abundance of such music suitable for children. Examples: *The Clavecin Book of Anna Magdalena Bach, Beethoven Sonatinas, Mozart Dances and Variations, Schubert Dances and Rondos.* These will lead into the larger Sonata forms as a natural sequence.

3. Attractive programmatic pieces. These must offer definite musical values besides having imaginative titles which will stimulate the student's creative expression. Look for clearly defined form, appealing melodic line, sound rhythmic patterns and good harmonic structure. Above all, try to find pieces which possess that indefinable quality—charm. Schumann, Grieg, Gretchaninoff, Tchaikovsky, etc. The works of these so-called romantic composers call for subjective interpretation. Besides their musical appeal, they should be geared to the technical and emotional limitations of the young student.

4. Technical studies which are short and concise and which exhibit a clearly defined purpose. They must be related in difficulty to the other compositions studied at the time. Those which emphasize scale and arpeggio patterns are the most useful.

5. The less complicated compositions of contemporary composers. Use these pieces experimentally. If your pupil rejects them, as he well may, do not be dismayed. Do not force the issue if he says they are ugly and sound queer. This reaction is understandable since his musical experience probably has been limited thus far to classical and popular music. His ear has been tuned to consonances, not dissonances. This distaste can be compared to the acquired taste for olives which many children dislike at first, only to enjoy them at a later date. A benign diet is normal for

the young child. Gentle exposure to the idiom of modern music is the surest way to create interest and enjoyment.

6. The simpler compositions of Bach, such as *The Little Preludes*, the *Inventions*, only when the pupil has reached some degree of maturity. We cannot expect a young person of moderate gifts to grasp or to successfully interpret the more advanced works. Any attempt to force him at too early a date is sure to lead to failure. He may under compulsion master the technical difficulties, but the musical performance will be lifeless and without meaning. An even more serious and lasting result lies in the aversion that he may form to the very name of Bach. Many adults carry this prejudice throughout life. They thus deprive themselves of what might have been their richest experience, because of misdirection in childhood. We must be cautious that we do not let our own preferences overshadow the child's. Appreciation of the heights in music arrives slowly. Our personal influence must be used with subtlety.

8. Chopin. There is no composer with a wider and more popular appeal, but a common error lies in the presenting of his compositions at too early a date. Young people often seek out brilliant pieces they have heard and attempt to play them, with a resultant failure. Besides the difficulties of technique, the emotional expression demanded for a true interpretation, except for a few waltzes and preludes, is highly sophisticated. The exception may be found in the highly talented child who demonstrates an understanding beyond his years in many areas. Adolescence, with its expanding emotions, is often the right time for the introduction of Chopin. Through a careful survey of all his works, a series can be made which will by gradual degrees lead to the most intricate and profound of his works.

20. Music for the Handicapped

> And whenever the evil spirit from God was upon Saul, David took the lyre and played it with his hand, so Saul was refreshed, and was well, and the evil spirit departed from him.
>
> Samuel 1:16

Plato has said, "Musical training is a more potent instrument than any other, because rhythm and harmony find their way into the inward places of the soul on which they mightily fasten, imparting grace." This ancient analysis could be used as a guide to music therapy, which is assuming an increasing importance in the treatment of the mentally ill and the retarded child. Progressive piano teachers may wish to keep abreast of the times by a knowledge of what is being accomplished in this challenging field, although a crowded teaching schedule may prevent active participation. Dedicated volunteers throughout the country are helping to carry on this valuable service though their numbers are pitifully inadequate in relation to the need.

Ten years ago, quite by chance, I heard Dr. T. Thayer Gaston speak on the topic of music therapy. Until that time I had considered my working hours to be completely filled with teaching, concerts, lectures, etc. His inspiring words caused me to enter on a period of self-examination, and I felt I must respond to his appeal to bring some form of music to a part of the tremendous number of hospitalized people in this country.

Dr. Gaston's pioneer work at the University of Kansas and in connection with the Menninger Clinic has firmly established the therapeutic value of music in the treatment of the mentally ill. Authentic data are available not only from the United States but also from Europe. The *Journal of the American Medical Association* and many other reputable magazines have published numerous articles proving without doubt that music can and does reach the patient lost in a world of isolation and despair.

It would be a false claim to say that music alone can cure a patient suffering from one of the many mental diseases. Though there are surprising cases of recovery on record, it must be kept in mind that many therapies are used simultaneously. Music should be thought of as a valuable tool whose potentialities have never been fully explored. All signs point to a rich field for future development.

Music therapy is not concerned with psychiatric hospitals alone. It can be used with benefit for all long-term hospitalized patients. The prospective therapist is free to choose the field best suited to his temperament and interest. However, since every second hospital bed is occupied by a mental patient, the greatest need for music is in this area.

I began my career in music therapy by serving as a volunteer in one of the large psychiatric state hospitals. This was a valuable if rugged experience. I was untrained and filled with fears and self doubts. I gradually emerged from this unhappy state by constant study of available literature pertaining to the subject and by practical experience with all kinds of patients. The discovery that music could reach them soon gave me great satisfaction, which continues to the present day.

After one year I was appointed to the staff of Ingleside

Psychiatric Hospital as music therapist. The immediate problem was a question of time. How was it possible to add a daily hospital stint to a seemingly full schedule of teaching and conservatory duties? This was solved by the allotting of an early morning hour in which I conducted a chorus for the patients. Treatments of various kinds are given in the morning and through music the attention is diverted from the ordeal ahead. I use a wide variety of songs of a popular and light nature, occasional hymns if they are requested, and many old and familiar selections. The patients make their own choice of what they wish to sing. Sometimes a forgotten song from childhood will penetrate their silence. A new arrival may at first be reluctant even to enter the room but is drawn in later as he hears the others singing. Once the song book is accepted certain steps are sure to follow. At first he may merely look at the words; next, say them softly; but after a few days, is heard singing.

A warm personal relationship between therapist and patient is of prime importance and is not difficult to establish provided the therapist approaches his task with an affectionate understanding. Withdrawn and even hostile patients can be drawn into the group eventually if the proper technique is learned. Doctors, nurses, and attendants join in the singing from time to time. Birthday songs are sung, and there is always a farewell tune when the happy day arrives for discharge. At this time I have heard the same sentence repeated again and again, "Music was the one thing which seemed to come through to me. I shall never forget this morning hour."

I often find amateur or even professional musicians among the group. These are encouraged to sing solos, duets, or even to play their own instruments as their improvement permits. Monthly concerts by outside talent are a special feature of the therapy program. I spend all holidays such as Christmas, Thanksgiving, etc., with my patients for these are the periods of greatest stress and the times when music is most needed. What are the benefits to be derived from group participation in singing? They are manifold. Self-respect and a feeling of comradeship are engendered. The solitary, frightened patient gradually comes to realize that he "belongs." Friendships are formed through this daily assembling, and the improved patient often gives comfort and encouragement to the new arrival. I constantly ask for help in arranging chairs, passing out books, etc. Through assisting me the patient is given the salutary feeling of being needed.

Authorities tell us that the primitive quality of non-verbal language lies in music. Only now are we beginning to practice what was known by savage tribes who revered their "medicine man." Drums, crude instruments, and incantations were used to drive out the evil spirits believed to be the cause of disease. David playing on his harp to Saul (who was doubtless a victim of schizophrenia) presents a well known example of music therapy. The ancient Greeks held music in high regard and used it freely in the treatment of all diseases. Hippocrates set down exact tables of disease-symptoms and musical treatment. For example, a bilious temperament indicating gall bladder trouble was treated by a soprano singing in the Phrygian mode.

This country's employment of music in hospitals stemmed from the first "World War" when the Veterans Administration was the leader in recognizing the therapeutic value of music for disabled veterans. Today there is a resident music therapist working full time in most government hospitals for the mentally ill. Many other signs indicate that increased attention is being given to this sadly neglected field.

This brief account of the progress of music therapy for the mentally ill presents only one of the many possibilities inherent in the use of music. If you are a piano teacher in semi-retirement, or one with some leisure hours at your command, I suggest that you explore the local situation. You will without doubt discover opportunities for the use of your talent in many areas of social service.

If, however, you are reluctant to embark on an institutional project, I am very sure that sooner or later you will find another vexing situation at your door. What of the physically handicapped child? There are many intelligent children with varying degrees of musical aptitude or talent who have a keen desire to play the piano but who are hampered by some physical defect. Are they to be denied the privilege of self-expression or are there ways and means of overcoming such difficult obstacles? I firmly believe that the answer is YES, if we are prepared to give this question intensive study. Infinite patience and an active imagination are the necessary essentials with which to begin.

I have recently made a survey of my colleagues at The Cleveland Institute of Music and with very few exceptions found that many teachers had encountered a variety of problems pertaining to the physical structure of the body, particularly the hand and arm. In addition there are many physical diseases which would seem to exclude the study of an instrument. A fascinating and useful dossier could be compiled of their combined experiences and the attempted solutions. The most practical approach I can offer is to tell you of the situations I have encountered in my own class of piano students and my attempts to find a workable solution.

One of my most gifted pupils, who showed brilliant promise at the age of six, had fifty per cent vision. It was necessary to enlarge the notes and fingerings in order for him to read from the page. His mother gave me most able help in this necessary but time-consuming activity. At the age of seven he was run over by a speeding car and his right leg was amputated. His eagerness to return to the piano never abated during the long months of convalescence. It was the main point of discussion during the many visits I made to him in the hospital. I gave him a piano lesson on the first day we were given the doctor's permission after his return home. From that time on he was my outstanding pupil for nine years. You may well ask, "What of the pedals? How is it possible to reach a virtuoso level without their full use?" Since even with an artificial limb he could not use his right foot for the sustaining pedal, he learned to substitute with his left, thereby being deprived completely of the other pedals. Because of this seemingly insurmountable obstacle he developed a most beautiful pianissimo through the use of the fingers alone. It is quite possible that were you to hear him today you would be unaware of his handicap. He is now a performing artist of the highest calibre and is a full professor at a leading university.

The mental attitude of handicapped children is sure to be affected by the difficulties and frustrations they must encounter. We must be careful to offer empathy—not sympathy with its weakening and over-emotional implications. If we can obtain the parent's full cooperation and meet this challenge frankly, restraining our natural feeling of pity, the handicapped child can be given a fair chance of exploring music if he so desires. Humor must be cultivated. This student has experienced sorrow and needs the lift sure to come if music lessons are made joyous events. At the same time he must not be treated as an invalid and excused from the discipline required in any serious study of music. This would do him grave injustice. We should proceed as naturally as possible. Every afflicted person, if he has not been made neurotic by misguided parents and teachers, wishes to be treated as a normal human being.

I have also taught a child suffering from cerebral palsy. She was brought to me at the age of nine. Her interest in music was very keen and she wanted above all else to play the piano. Her family assumed that this was an impossible desire and had wisely provided her with a rich background of music recordings. She had also been taken to many concerts and showed a surprising knowledge of music for her age. However, these musical activities did not satisfy her for she longed to produce, not only listen to music. She was being given physiotherapy treatments and her doctor suggested piano lessons simply for the exercise of the fingers. This points up the need for close cooperation between the teacher and the physician or his medical co-workers.

I discovered at the first interview that this student had perfect pitch and could sing beautifully though she was slightly deaf. Her bodily movements were spastic. She could only strike the piano with her whole hand. The fingers were almost completely immobile. It appeared to be a hopeless situation. I tried to conceal this depressing fact from her and turned her attention to theory—intervallic and chordal relationships, ear training, solfege, rhythmic exercises such as clapping and conducting, which she could do with large though uncoordinated movements. She could read music from the staff, and the location of notes on the piano was quickly mastered. I encouraged her to compose simple melodies which I wrote down from her dictation. This project was continued during the four years she was with me.

We finally approached the playing of the piano. All scale technique was obviously impossible. I taught her to play successive notes using her whole hand and she was eventually able to play two notes together. In spite of the extremely difficult problem of coordination she had as assets a very fine understanding of rhythm and an almost mature grasp of the musical content. The material chosen had to be geared to her capacity. She had great pleasure in playing duets with me since only one line of melody is required. I made special arrangements of the music she loved, simplifying and reducing the chordal content to the minimum. Muscle tone and co-ordination improved under the daily piano practice and her doctor was delighted with her physical progress. This girl will have through life the ability to play simple forms of music for her own enjoyment as well as a superior equipment for listening.

I am often asked about teaching the blind. This lot may fall to any piano teacher, and it is well to be prepared. I have graduated two blind students from my own school, each taking a Bachelor's Degree, one in piano, the other a Master's in theory and composition. Both are now leading successful lives as teachers. Schools for the blind are always in need of qualified piano teachers, and there are many opportunities in the public schools for teaching blind or partially blind children. My two pupils are teaching in institutions of both kinds.

I felt very much at a loss when, many years ago, the first

blind student was assigned me. I knew nothing about this painful handicap and was very apprehensive as to methods. A visit to the American Foundation for the Blind in New York City was an invaluable experience. There I gained considerable insight from the director who gave me simple basic rules to observe: "Never lead a blind person—let him take your arm. Strive constantly to develop his own independence. He must have a Braille watch and not be required to ask the time. Encourage him to go to his classes alone after showing him the route."

Since all the music learned had to be in Braille, and many of the scores were outdated and miserably edited, much extra time had to be given to checking the correct notes. There is a great need for volunteers in this field, to enlarge and improve music literature in Braille for the blind. The plastic molding of the hand was the simplest part of the lesson, for the blind person is of necessity remarkably sensitive to touch. The law of compensation is always at work, and one sense will take over and become highly developed when another is missing. The ear becomes doubly alert to sound when there is no sight. I encouraged the use of recordings and did much playing for the pupil in order to develop proper interpretations. A blind person must be given many hours of teaching outside the regular schedule. The obstacles are many, but so are the rewards. There can be no finer opportunity for service than to help in the development of a talent which is beset with handicaps. We have on our present faculty a member of the theory department who is totally blind. He is an accomplished musician and commands the respect and affection of all his students.

I am currently teaching a sixteen-year-old boy who has

had six operations for glaucoma. When he came to me six years ago his talent was apparent but he had been taught entirely by rote. His teacher had merely played for him and allowed the child to imitate him. Musical notation was unknown to him. I had to be very firm and insisted that he try to read from the staff by means of a special magnifying glass. This was the doctor's order. In cases such as this it is imperative that we have direct advice from the physician in charge. This lad has gradually overcome his inaccurate, careless, undisciplined habits, and now takes pride in his legitimate performance. The first months were spent in establishing a firm friendship without which I could not have enforced the necessary rigid rules so foreign to him. He now performs advanced classics most beautifully and has shown great talent for composition. I believe that a fine career in music is assured.

A promising new pupil once presented a most challenging problem. Halfway in a lesson he suddenly stopped playing, his hands resting motionless on the keys. After a few seconds he resumed the composition. I was puzzled but fortunately did not question him. The second time this occurred, I knew that consultation with the mother was necessary. She revealed the fact that the child was suffering from petit mal, a mild form of epilepsy. Further advice from his doctor was encouraging. This disease is often outgrown as the child matures. I was told that my attitude should be hopeful and encouraging, and that I must avoid all pressure. Children who have this disease must be guarded from emotional excitement as their nervous susceptibility is of a high degree.

What of children with an infirmity following polio? Again the piano can be played without the use of the pedals if the legs are in braces. Should the arms be too deeply affected to use at the piano, theory can be studied and perhaps the drums suggested as a means of rhythmic expression. The child who has an active interest in music should be provided some kind of outlet. If a handicap makes his choice impossible, a substitute should be offered. This theory applies to many injuries of the hand. The recorder, flute and clarinet are sometimes possible when the technique required for the piano cannot be obtained.

There are many other disabilities too numerous to be categorized. I have known a child with a very short fifth finger who was unable to play octaves. The solution? Omit the octave, substituting another note from the chord, which can be played by a normal finger. Materials must be most carefully chosen and by constant searching for new and old compositions it is possible to find those which present the least difficulties. It is tremendously important in teaching a handicapped person to know in advance what will be impossible for him to perform, thus saving him needless frustration.

One of the piano teachers in my department reported a student with one arm considerably shorter than the other. This created an awkward posture as the body had to be turned to provide the proper coordination between the hands. Considerable ingenuity was required but by trial and error a reasonable position was established with the minimum of tension.

Tension is an ever present enemy when we are working against a handicap. Physical exercises away from the piano are advisable to create easy arm and shoulder movements. I ask the pupil to stop several times during each lesson or practice session, to stand up and rotate the full arm, thereby freeing the muscles from the cramped position they have assumed. Other exercises can be invented according to the needs of the student. A comfortable chair with a cushion at the back is a desirable substitute for the rigid and backless bench.

I shall not attempt to discuss in detail the remarkable work that is being done with music for retarded children in many schools throughout the country since I have not had the time nor opportunity to participate in this fairly recent development.

I am told that professional workers are all too few and without the invaluable aid of volunteers the program would fall by the wayside. I have witnessed many demonstrations held with these deprived children and am amazed and heartened by the results obtained. Their response was enthusiastic and their love for the teacher most apparent. One of my very fine adult piano students has volunteered her services and tells me that it is the most rewarding thing she has ever done. This may well be an activity quickly at hand if you are a piano teacher who feels the urge to use your music in some form of social service. Simple nursery and action songs are played and the children given every encouragement to participate. You must of course love children and be able to extend this love to include the little retarded child. You may discover that your own musical life has been infinitely enriched and enlarged.

There are many more needs than the few I have mentioned. I have held music programs at the Florence Crittenton Home, the Rehabilitation Center at Mt. Sinai Hospital, and the polio ward at City Hospital. The opportunities are all about us if we but search.

The situations discussed in this chapter are taken from

actual experience. Any qualified teacher of piano who has taught many years could without doubt verify in part or add to these personal statements. It is impossible to separate the teaching of the piano from the problems and even tragedies which may come to our door. George Herbert Palmer states:

> Most human beings are contented with living one life and delighted if they can pass that agreeably. But this is not enough for us teachers. We incessantly go outside ourselves and enter into the many lives about us,—lives dull, dark, and unintelligible to any but an eye like ours. And this is imagination, the sympathetic creation in ourselves of conditions which belong to others.

This is perhaps too lofty a goal but we would do well to enlarge the scope of our vision and attempt to understand more of the human being entrusted to our care, his needs and infirmities as well as his talent. Proficient as we may be in our own specialized field of the piano we must look into related areas if we are to fulfill our true vocation of musical guide and counselor.

21. Holiday Party

> The old year now away is fled,
> The new year it is entered;
> Then let us now our sins down-tread,
> And joyfully all appear:
> Let's be merry this day,
> And let us now both sport and play:
> Hang grief, cast care away.
> God send you a Happy New Year.
>
> Greensleeves

The Christmas season produces an outpouring of carols which would seem to be the prerogative of singers. Piano teachers usually exclude themselves from participation in this activity. This need not be the case if we are alert to new ways in which the piano may be used. The festive atmosphere surrounding the holidays, beloved by children, provides a delightful incentive for a Christmas Musicale. The countless beautiful carols at our command can be played as well as sung.

The first requirement is a careful study of the wealth of available material, both familiar and unknown. A list of useful collections of carols will be found at the end of this chapter. Each teacher is free to make his own choice in the assembling of the program, but I suggest that he not lean too heavily upon the tried and true carols, many of which have become hackneyed by over-use. Their delicate beauty is destroyed by constant repetition and the blaring of loud-

Holiday Party 139

speakers in shops and supermarkets. This annoying racket is anti-climactic since it starts long before the true period of celebration which should be in the days just preceding Christmas.

Carols from many lands are to be found if we do research in this fascinating field. We need not confine ourselves to English carols alone. It is a rewarding labor to lift a carol from obscurity and give it life once more. A study of the history of the carol brings to light many interesting facts and provides an authentic key to their interpretation. We soon discover that they were danced as well as sung. The very word "carol" probably derives from the Greek "choros" which meant to dance in a ring. Processionals abound in pictorial art and we see groups of singers accompanied by instruments of various kinds, pipes or flutes, horns, lutes, drums, etc. The prevailing spirit was gaiety. Unfortunately this tradition was discarded in the seventeenth century. Puritanism frowned upon any celebration of Christmas Day, which in one published tract was called "The Old Heathen's Feasting Day." Any music that was allowed was without doubt lugubrious and gloomy. Yet St. Paul in his doctrines anticipated the familiar words, "Love and joy come to you." It is a cause for rejoicing that we have returned to this original conception of Christmas music.

The true carol sprang from the people and portrayed the natural instincts of joy and wonder. St. Francis of Assisi is said to have been the first caroler. He danced and sang in the joy of his faith. *The Oxford Book of English Carols* defines them as "songs with a religious impulse that are simple, hilarious, popular, and buoyant even when the subject is a grave one." These qualities are universal in their appeal to both children and adults. Fortified by the knowledge of this earlier conception, the piano teacher is equipped to translate the sung carol to the medium of the piano. We can put these lovely melodies to good use in the teaching of beautiful tone production.

As Christmas approaches it is pleasant to acquaint our children with some of the many legends concerning this ancient festival; the reasons for the use of our familiar decorations—holly, evergreens, mistletoe, the Christmas tree, etc. However, some myths may well be omitted since they stem from pagan rites and are apt to be too lurid in tone for childish imaginations.

Mistletoe was put to various uses including a humorous one which children will enjoy. You must hang a wreath of it around the neck of the first cow you meet on New Year's Day or its milk will turn sour and you will have bad luck. Holly must be burned on the twelfth night following Christmas or again you will be in trouble.

The custom of burning candles on Christmas Eve is widespread. Some authorities believe it to have originated in Ireland where even today one sees a lighted candle in the front window of most homes. This is symbolic of lighting the Holy Family on its night travels.

The story of the first creche originated by St. Francis is a special favorite. The creche and the nativity figures which surrounded it were of giant size. It was placed in the public square around which St. Francis and his followers danced, singing praises to the Lord.

Children also love the story of the first Christmas tree. Martin Luther was walking and praying in the dark woods one Christmas Eve. Looking up to the stars shining through the fir trees he was moved to bring a pine tree into the house. Burning candles were placed upon it to simulate for his children the wonder of God's forests and heavens. This custom was gradually adopted through the continent and after many years found its way into England and eventually to America.

Carols met with a sorry fate in the Puritan days of our own New England. The state of Maine in 1695 levied a five shilling tax on anyone found guilty of feasting, caroling, or staying away from work on Christmas day. I suggest to my children that they should not be too demanding in their own Christmas requests since they are singularly fortunate to be living now, rather than then.

The most familiar carol of all, "Silent Night," carries a charming story. It was written in 1818 by Franz Gruber, organist of a little church in Oberndorf, Austria. One Christmas Eve he found to his dismay that the organ was out of order and could not be used for the Christmas morning service. Thinking that a new hymn might help the situation, he asked the Pastor Joseph Mohr to write verses which Gruber then set to music, working through the night. He sang it the next morning to the accompaniment of a guitar. This was the first performance of "Silent Night." Another surprise is the discovery that "We Three Kings of Orient Are," which one assumes was imported from England, was written by the Rev. John Henry Hopkins of Williamsport, Pennsylvania.

Some part of this interesting history can be explained to our students as the Christmas program is in preparation. This is an annual event long anticipated with great pleasure by my piano class. It is always held the Sunday before

Christmas. A crowded teaching schedule often prevents intimate gatherings in which a family is included. A Christmas recital provides a golden opportunity for teachers to meet fathers since both parents are invited. They may witness not only the progress of their own child, but can observe as well what other children are accomplishing. They are all anxious for their children to play well and a pleasurable excitement prevails.

I send out gay invitations well in advance and decorate my house with evergreens, holly, balloons, candles, candy canes, and small gifts to be distributed at the close of the afternoon. I find most children to be highly conventional. They want everything in its place just as it was the preceding year. The continuity of this event gives it a dynamic force and sets a musical goal for the piano lessons months before the musicale. I am often asked the question early in September, "What will I play at the Christmas party?" It takes only the first party to create an eagerness for the second and an ambition to make progress.

What part does the carol play in the Christmas recital? Since I use all the children in my class, their ages ranging from seven to sixteen, the program is divided into two parts with the small ones in the first section. This is entitled "Holiday Music," which is obviously the place for the simple carols.

Years ago when this project was first started, I used the heading "Christmas Music." I was disturbed by the fact that the Jewish children did not know the carols used and were silent during the carol singing in which the parents were asked to join and which always follows the program. It occurred to me to explore the songs used for the Jewish

Hanukkah (The Festival of Lights) which takes place just before Christmas. This holiday ranks high in importance in the Jewish faith and is widely celebrated in many countries.

Hanukkah originated in 165 B.C. to commemorate the victory of Judas Maccabeus over the Greco-Syrian invaders of Israel. The festival lasts eight days and is a joyous period. Gifts are exchanged and special games are played by the children, one in particular in which a spinning top of clay (dreidl) is used. A song is sung as it spins. Other traditional songs appropriate to the occasion are sung by young and old. The shamus or master candle is used to light the first candle of the seven-branched minorah and another candle lit each successive night until all are burning on the eighth or last night. I found that my Jewish students all knew "My Dreidl," "Rock of Ages," "Hanukkah Pancakes," etc. I then made simple arrangements of these melodies and included them with the Christmas carols both played and sung. The result has been the most happy mingling of several faiths, Catholic, Protestant, and Jewish. Differences of race and religion are forgotten and in this hour music is the catalyst which cancels out prejudice and discord.

In the search for interesting carols I have explored collections from many countries, discovering many rare songs often unknown. I include these with the familiar, plus the Hanukkah songs. Negro spirituals, which are our own American heritage, offer some of the most poignant carols.

The great advantage in making our own piano arrangements lies in the fact that they can be geared to the ability of the individual child. If he is a beginner I choose songs with the simplest rhythmic pattern comparable to the folk tunes found in his beginning books. I copy out the melody and add a slight harmonic background of chords.

The entire first half of the program is presented in duet form. I remain at the piano playing the bass part to give moral and rhythmic support. These are the youngest children, who may be experiencing their first public performance, and I never allow them to be alone. Failure is practically impossible with the teacher close at hand to supply a remedy quickly, should the child falter or lose his place. We must prevent at all costs any trauma resulting from an apparent failure.

An interesting enlargement of my Christmas musicale in recent years has been the inclusion of instruments other than the piano. By questioning we may discover a brother or sister, or the piano student himself who plays in a school band or orchestra. Last year I was able to find two violins, a flute, a clarinet, and a harp, all of which contributed greatly to the color of the program.

A small stairway in my house is used for an opening processional. Bells are rung on the stroke of three o'clock, which is the signal for the children to start down the stairs singing "Deck the Halls with Boughs of Holly." The extra instruments add an obligato and are also used later in the program in solos and duets.

The second half of the program consists of classic compositions and proceeds chronologically as to difficulty. The closing numbers are obviously the most advanced and should be of a brilliant nature which presents an enticing goal for the younger children. Since all grades are represented, the pattern of development can be observed by both parents and children. This particular recital affords them a unique opportunity of both listening and performing. Their progress can be measured from year to year and their personal ambition stimulated.

If you are a piano teacher handicapped by a small apartment or house, this need not be an insuperable problem. I held my first Christmas recital in a tiny apartment with a handful of guests. My present house is small, but by moving furniture and calling to my aid the services of a friendly undertaker, glad to contribute chairs, it can be made to hold a surprising number of guests. No one minds a bit of crowding at such a time.

I have established a pleasant conclusion to the afternoon in the form of a farewell to a student who is graduating from high school in the current year, and who will therefore be taking part in his last Christmas musicale. A gift is presented from the piano class and a little speech made by one of the children. This is a very touching ceremony and one eagerly awaited by all. The recipient usually responds with impromptu words of appreciation, and it is not unusual to observe a few tears here and there, for this occasion marks the final participation in a beloved tradition. The departing student is now ready for college or conservatory study.

Community singing concludes the program. Then comes a highly important point in the afternoon. REFRESHMENTS. No children's party would be complete without this pleasant reward. Most parents are delighted to share in this activity and the over-worked teacher is eased of a burden. The children all gather around me at the piano and sing holiday songs of their choosing while a committee of parents removes the extra chairs to the basement and sets up the punch table. In a few moments all is made ready for the hilarious confusion sure to break forth. Numbers have ceased to alarm me for I have entertained as many as seventy at such a gathering. Careful planning and an allocation of duties to willing parents solves most difficulties.

Exciting rewards await the teacher attempting such an undertaking for the first time. The aftermath of appreciation and happiness lasts far into the new year. Lazy or reluctant students may be inspired to greater efforts, the talented ones to a higher goal. The tired teacher reviewing the afternoon after her guests have departed, will know with surety that for a few hours the true spirit of Christmas prevailed.

* * *

Holiday Music

Carols from Green Duet Book	Diller and Page	Schirmer
Carols from Brown Duet Book	Diller and Page	Schirmer
Merry Christmas	Walter Kirby	Willis
Jolly Christmas Melodies	Irene Rodgers	Willis
Christmas Carols	Irene Rodgers	Willis
Carol Book	Diller and Page	Schirmer
Let Us Have Music for Christmas	Maxwell Eckstein	Carl Fischer
Christmas Carols	Mary Bacon Mason	Oliver Ditson
Christmas in Song	Theodore Preuss	Rubank
Pianist's Christmas Book	Stanley Fletcher	Summy-Birchard
Christmas Eve—Medley	Harold C. Cobb	Summy-Birchard
Greensleeves	Louise Rebe	Summy-Birchard
Little Christmas Fantasy	Preston Orem	Summy-Birchard
Noel	Balbastre-Ohl	Summy-Birchard

Source Collections for Piano Arrangements

Favorite Christmas Carols	Norman Lloyd	Simon and Schuster
Christmas Carols from Many Countries	Coleman and Jurgensen	Schirmer
Oxford Book of Christmas Carols		Oxford Press
Songs of Zion	Harry Coopersmith	Block Publishing Co.

Sources and Acknowledgments

I wish to acknowledge my deep indebtedness to the late Arthur Loesser whose constant encouragement and inestimable advice were instrumental in the writing of this book. My fervent gratitude also goes to Dr. Allan Nevins, who was good enough to read my manuscript and whose valuable suggestions I have followed faithfully. I am under special obligation to Nan Giesey for wise counsel and exceptional kindness in addition to her professional services.

The Research Department of the Cleveland Public Library was diligent in helping to locate the source of materials used, some of which were out of print. They were unfailing in courtesy and patience.

Clavier, Evanston, Illinois, has kindly given permission to use various articles which I have written for past issues.

I thank Houghton Mifflin Company, Boston, for permission to reprint quotations from *The Ideal Teacher* by George Herbert Palmer and *Looking Backward* by Edward Bellamy. Also I thank Mrs. John Holmes for "In a Classroom" by John Holmes, E. P. Dutton & Co., Inc. for *Conversations with Casals* by J. Ma. Corredor translated by André Mangeot, and Harper for *The Web and the Rock* by Thomas Wolfe.

Bibliography

Amiel, Henry Frederic. *Journal.* Translated by Mrs. Humphrey Ward. Macmillan

Arnold, Matthew. *Collected Poems.* Dutton

Bellamy, Edward. *Looking Backward.* Houghton Mifflin

Bible (King James Version)

Casals, Pablo. *Conversations with Casals.* By J. Ma. Corredor. Dutton

Chaucer, Geoffrey. *Canterbury Tales.* Oxford University Press

Chaucer, Geoffrey. *Parliament of Fowls.* Oxford University Press

Comenius, John Amos. *The Great Didactic.* Macmillan

Confucius. *The Wisdom of Confucius.* Translated by Lin Yutang. Modern Library

David, H. T. and Mendel, A. *The Bach Reader.* Norton

Donne, John. *Sermons.* Clarendon Press

Einstein, Alfred. *Mozart, His Life and Works.* Doubleday

Holmes, John. *Map of My Country.* Duell, Sloan and Pearce

James, William. *Talks to Teachers.* Modern Library

Loesser, Arthur. *Men, Women, and Pianos.* Simon and Schuster

Lyly, John. *Euphues.* Russell and Russell

Mann, Thomas. *Essays of Three Decades.* Knopf

Mendelssohn, Felix. *Collected Letters.* Edited by G. Selden-Goth. Pantheon

Montaigne, Michel de. *Selected Essays.* Translated by W. C. Hazlitt. Modern Library

Oxford Book of Carols. Oxford University Press

Palmer, George Herbert. *The Ideal Teacher.* Houghton Mifflin

Plato. *Dialogues of Plato.* Translated by Benjamin Jowett. Boni and Liveright

Quiller-Couch, Sir Arthur. *On the Art of Reading.* Putnam

Rousseau, Jean Jacques. *Emile.* Translated by Barbara Foxley. Dutton

Schumann, Robert. *Maxims for Young Musicians.* McGraw Hill

Slenczynski, Ruth. *Lost Childhood.* Viking

Thompson, Francis. *Essay on Shelley. Dublin Review,* July 1908

Wierznski, Casimir. *Life of Chopin.* Translated by Norbert Guterman. Simon and Schuster

Whitehead, Alfred North. *Dialogues.* Recorded by Lucien Price. Little, Brown

Wolfe, Thomas. *The Web and the Rock.* Harper